AIRPORT SPOTT

CW00544899

UNITED KINGDOM & IRELAND

DestinWorld
publishing

First Edition 2016
ISBN 978-0-9955307-1-3

British Library Cataloguing-in-Publication Data

A catalogue record for this book is available from the British Library.

Published by Destinworld Publishing Ltd.

www.destinworld.com

Cover Design by John Wright

All photographs © Matthew Falcus

Table of Contents

UK and Ireland Airport Statistics

Top 10 Busiest UK & Ireland Airports by Passengers

Rank		2015 Passengers
1	London Heathrow	74,985,748
2	London Gatwick	40,269,087
3	Dublin	25,049,335
4	Manchester	23,136,047
5	London Stansted	22,519,178
6	London Luton	12,263,505
7	Edinburgh	11,114,587
8	Birmingham	10,187,122
9	Glasgow	8,714,307
10	Bristol	6,786,790

Top 10 Busiest UK & Ireland Airports by Movements

Rank		2015 Movements
1	London Heathrow	474,087
2	London Gatwick	267,760
3	Dublin	191,233
4	Manchester	173,165
5	London Stansted	168,629
6	Edinburgh	115,286
7	London Luton	114,083
8	Aberdeen	112,357
9	Birmingham	98,015
10	Glasgow	90,790

Top 10 Largest UK & Ireland Airlines

Rank		Fleet Size
1	Ryanair	337
2	British Airways	294
3	easyJet	247
4	Flybe	76
5	Thomson Airways	64
6	Jet2.com	56
7	Aer Lingus	45
8	Virgin Atlantic	40
9	Monarch	34
10	Thomas Cook Airlines	32

Top 10 Longest UK & Ireland Runways

Rank	Airport	Length
1	London Heathrow	12,802ft / 3,902m
2	London Heathrow	12,008ft / 3,660m
3	London Gatwick	10,879ft / 3,316m
4	MoD Boscombe Down	10,538ft / 3,212m
5	Birmingham	10,013ft / 3,052m
6	Manchester	10,007ft / 3,050m
7	London Stansted	10,003ft / 3,049m
8	Manchester	10,000ft / 3,048m
9	RAF Fairford	9,990ft / 3,045m
10	Bruntingthorpe	9,843ft / 3,000m

England

Birmingham

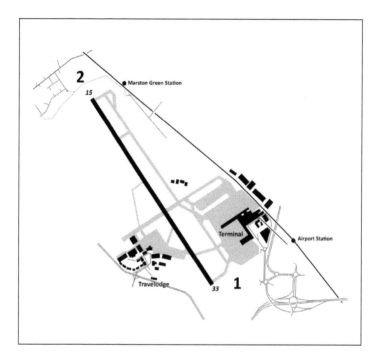

Runways
15/33 10,013ft / 3,052m

Hub For: Flybe, Jet2, Monarch, Ryanair, Thomas Cook Airlines, Thomson Airways

The airport gateway to England's second city has been growing in stature in recent years with a number of based low cost airlines, and ever more long haul links. At face value Birmingham doesn't offer much more than can be found at Manchester or London's main airports, but it is worth a visit when in the area. Aside from the heavy presence of Flybe, Jet2, Monarch, Ryanair, Thomas Cook and Thomson, other carriers of note include Emirates with at least one daily Airbus A380, United Airlines Qatar Airways, Norwegian, Pakistan International, Turkish, Turkmenistan Airlines and Wizz Air. Europe's full service carriers are also well represented, including Aer Lingus, Air France, Brussels Airlines, KLM, Lufthansa, Swiss and Scandinavian Airlines. The presence of seasonal services to China in recent years suggests a permanent link may not be far off.

Birmingham's modern terminal occupies the south western portion of the site, with two piers (the former British Airways 'EuroHub' is now home to Flybe and Ryanair predominantly). Across the runway is the former Elmdon Airport and its historic terminal. Today biz jets and cargo airliners park here, alongside Monarch's maintenance hangar which sometimes sees unusual visitors.

In terms of cargo, Birmingham sees FedEx Express, BinAir and West Atlantic turboprops nightly, with occasional charters by Russian types.

The viewing gallery and aviation shop are sadly long gone, so spotters need to find alternative arrangements. Spotters often enjoy taking video and pictures of aircraft struggling with the prevalent crosswinds at Birmingham.

SPOTTING LOCATIONS

1. Long Stay Car Park

The airport provides an official viewing area in the Long Stay Car Park alongside the runway 33 threshold and taxiway. There are benches and a good view of aircraft movements through the fence, and shortly before touchdown. Follow signs from the terminal.

2. Runway 15

At the northern end of the airport this spot is good for approach and crosswind photographs. A path here runs across the approach path. It is best accessed from Hazeldene Road (postcode B33 0QB), off The Radleys. If you're heading from Birmingham city centre, follow the A45 and then turn left onto Sheaf Lane in Sheldon. This turns into

Church Road. After a mile turn right onto The Radleys, and right again opposite the car garage. Alternatively, get the train to Marston Green station (one stop from the airport/NEC) and walk along the path to the viewing area.

HOTELS

Travelodge Birmingham Airport

Terminal Road, Birmingham B26 3QW |
+44 871 984 6483 | www.travelodge.co.uk

Located on the old terminal side of the airport, rooms facing the airport on the top two floors have great views across the runway and to the passenger terminal. You can't see the executive and cargo ramp, but will see all movements. This is now the only acceptable place to spot around the old terminal building, as security will move you on if they see you loitering outside.

Blackbushe

Runways
07/25 4,380ft / 1,335m

It's hard to imagine today that, after World War II, Blackbushe became one of London's two primary civil airports handling flights from around the world. This ended in the early 1960s when the airport reopened as a general aviation facility. Today it is fairly busy with light aircraft and sees a good mix of executive aircraft visiting.

Blackbushe has one runway, with an area of grass and concrete parking at the south east corner of the site, next to the small handling facilities.

Most aircraft can be seen from the fence next to the car park outside the control tower. A short walk along the fence line next to the A30 road should yield anything missing.

Public Transport: Blackbushe is around 5 miles from Farnborough, and 23 miles from Heathrow Airport. There are no public transport links to the airport, but railway stations in Farnborough and Blackwater are fairly close.

Blackpool

Runways
10/28 6,132ft / 1,869m
13/31 3,294ft / 1,004m

Blackpool Airport has had mixed fortunes in recent years, going from a busy regional airport with based aircraft of Jet2, to closure in 2014. Thankfully the airport was reopened in April 2015 and has since been undergoing redevelopment of the site and business model. Scheduled flights to the Isle of Man are once again on offer, with Citywing LET 410s. Helicopter services to Irish Sea oil rigs and general aviation make up the majority of movements.

Blackpool has two active runways, with all service buildings running along Squires Gate Lane which runs from the nearby sea front. It's possible to see parked aircraft from gaps between the hangars, and also from the fence line behind the Morrissons supermarket a little further along. Some operators are known to allow people to visit the hangars during quieter periods.

Public Transport: Buses #11 and #68 stop nearby the airport, linking it with the town centre. Bus #7 also runs along Squire's Gate Lane.

Bournemouth

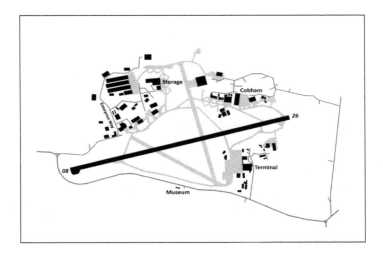

Runways

08/26 7,451ft / 2,271m

Hub For: Ryanair, Thomson Airways

Bournemouth Hurn is one of the busier airports in the South West of the country. For years it was a manufacturing plant for airliners such as the BAC One-Eleven and Vickers Viscount. Today a good amount of maintenance work still goes on, so it's usual to see some airliners and other aircraft parked outside the hangars on the north side.

Airliner traffic has been up and down. Most flights are with Ryanair's Boeing 737s as one of the airline's smaller hubs. Thomson Airways add seasonal services to the mix.

The airport is split into three distinct segments, separated by the main east-west runway and former cross runways. At the south east corner is the passenger terminal, apron and car parks. It is possible to follow the road here until you reach the perimeter fence and view aircraft parked in the Cobham areas and around the terminal, but don't loiter.

In the north east are flying clubs, air ambulance and a large facility operated by Cobham in conjunction with its Durham Tees Valley base. A drive along Mountbatten Drive (postcode BH23 6NE) will offer some glimpses through the fence.

The north west corner comprises many hangars and buildings associated with maintenance, storage, business aircraft, a Pilatus PC-12 centre, and non-aviation businesses. Enterprise Way (postcode BH23 6BS) is the main road running through this business park, and you are free to pass through the security post. Work your way past the various small roads running to different areas and spot what you can through the fence. At the end you'll come to the area used for airliner storage.

Public Transport: Bus #A1 links Bournemouth city centre with the airport passenger terminal. It also stops outside the museum (see below) and Enterprise Way in the north west section of the airport.

The **Bournemouth Aviation Museum** occupies a site off the B3073 on the southern perimeter. Open daily except Christmas bank holidays, with a selection of civil and military aircraft and cockpits. A double-decker bus here offers views across the airport from above the fence line. www.aviation-museum.co.uk

Brighton City Shoreham

Runways

02/20 3,399ft / 1,036m
02G/20G 2,297ft / 700m
07G/25G 2,877ft / 877m
13G/31G 1,339ft / 408m

Known mostly as Shoreham Airport, Brighton City is situated equidistant between Brighton and Worthing on a plain alongside the Rive Adur and the English Channel. It has one concrete runway and two grass runways, and is known as a centre for flight training. Its annual air show is also a highlight, despite the publicity caused by a fatal crash in 2015.

The airport does not have any passenger airline service, but has a lovely Art Deco terminal building in front of the aircraft parking apron and amongst the many small hangars running along the access road. Airside tours of the airport and hangars are offered from the Shoreham Airport Visitor Centre next to the terminal. Booking is advisable, see www.visitorcentre.info

The airport is used mostly by light aircraft, pleasure flights, helicopters and vintage aircraft. Follow Cecil Pashley Way past the terminal and you'll find a number of parking places along the fence line to watch movements from.

Public Transport: The nearest buses pass along the A259, and Shoreham railway station is a 20 minute walk from the airport.

Bristol

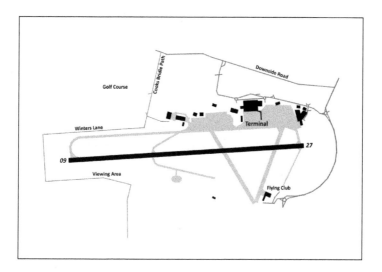

Runways

09/27 6,598ft / 2,011m

Hub For: bmi regional, easyJet, Ryanair, Thomas Cook Airlines, Thomson Airways

Bristol Airport is at Lulsgate, a few miles south of the city in South West England. It has a single runway and modern terminal and handled 6.7 million passengers in 2015. Passenger airliner parking aprons are found on the north side of the runway, which is in an east-west orientation. To the south light aircraft, executive aircraft and based flying clubs use parking areas on the former cross runways.

Bristol is a hub for bmi regional, easyJet, Ryanair and Thomson Airways. Other carriers include Aer Lingus Regional Aurigny, KLM Cityhopper, Thomas Cook Airlines, Wizz Air and WOW Air. The summer season sees many more charters and seasonal flights.

A dedicated spotting area exists at the Bristol and Wessex Aeroplane Club on the south side of the airport. Following the perimeter road from the terminal to the 'Silver Zone Car Park' and then find the club signposted. Views from the café here look across the runway to the terminal area.

Another popular location is Winters Lane. From the airport passenger terminal entrance, drive north on the A38 and take the first left along Downside Road. After a mile turn left along Cooks Bridle Path, signposted Tall Pines Golf Club. Pass the golf club and you'll reach the airport perimeter. Winters Lane follows this around the end of runway 09 to the south side where a car park offers views through the fence. Photography is difficult without a step ladder.

Public Transport: None of the spotting locations are accessible by public transport but can be walked from the passenger terminal. Regular buses link the terminal with Bristol city centre and train station.

RAF Brize Norton

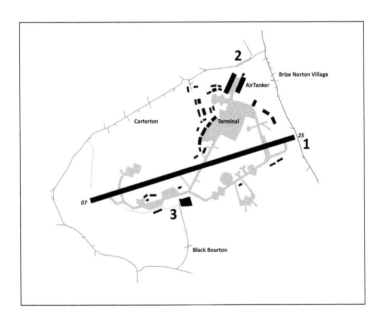

Runways
07/25 10,007ft / 3,050m

Hub For: Royal Air Force

Brize Norton in Oxfordshire is the Royal Air Force's principal air transport and air logistics base. It is home to the AirTanker fleet of Airbus A330 Voyagers, plus military parachuting and the air link to the Falkland Islands and Ascension. In addition the RAF's Hercules, A400M and C-17 fleets operate from here. Every week a variety of support aircraft, from biz jets to airliners and cargo aircraft, pass through.

The airfield has one runway running east-west with aprons and technical areas on both sides. The majority of the base, including the passenger terminal and AirTanker hangars are on the north side. Entering the base without a reason is generally not permitted, so any spotting needs to be done from outside the airfield.

SPOTTING LOCATIONS

1. Runway 25

One of the best locations for photography is the end of runway 25 where Station Road passes very close. You can't park here, so need to find a spot in Brize Norton village, or in the car park off Carterton Road (postcode OX18 3LY), which are a 10 minute and 20 minute walk respectively.

2. Carterton Road

Using this car park, you can walk along towards the large hangars at the base and grab fleeting views of any larger aircraft parked up here. Good for logging but not for photography.

3. Southern Perimeter

Head for Black Bourton village, and then follow Burdford Road (OX18 2PF) north until you reach the fence. Park here and then walk west along the track, stopping to pick off any aircraft parked on the southern dispersals and ramps.

Public Transport: Bus #S1 runs from nearby Oxford and Witney to Brize Norton village.

Bruntingthorpe

Runways

06/24 9,843ft / 3,000m
06R/24L 2,953ft / 900m

Not an airport as such, Bruntingthorpe is a former World War II airfield in rural Leicestershire which is now home to an interesting collection of preserved historic aircraft, and a storage/scrapping compound.

The Cold War Jets Open Days are a big draw to enthusiasts, where the collection of active aircraft are taken onto the runway for fast taxis. These are usually held a couple of times per year, but the museum is always open on a Sunday for viewing the aircraft (see www.bruntingthorpeaviation.com). Doing so gives you distant views of the stored aircraft on the airfield, which include former Olympic Airways and Transaero Boeing 747s and the Royal Air Force L1011 TriStar fleet.

Public Transport: Bus #661 from nearby Lutterworth (which is linked to long distance buses) passes the entrance to Bruntingthorpe.

Cambridge

Runways

05/23 6,446ft / 1,965m

A small airport on the eastern edge of the city. It has one concrete and two grass runways, with all of the aprons, hangars and other buildings on the north side of the site. Cambridge doesn't have any regular airline services, but does see plenty of airliner movements coming in for maintenance at Marshalls Aerospace, including RAF transport aircraft. Executive aircraft are also common.

Airport Way (head for Church Road, CB1 9AZ) runs along part of the eastern perimeter, with places to pull over and look across the airfield through the crash gates (don't obstruct).

At the southern end of the airport, a small residential street called Hatherdene Close (postcode CB1 3HQ) off Coldhams Lane has views across the runway to the Marshalls hangars.

Finally, at the northern part of the airfield you can park up near the flying club hangars and see some of the parked aircraft nearby.

Public Transport: Buses #10, 11 and 12 link the city centre with the airport and pass Airport Way. Bus #17 passes Hatherdene Close.

Carlisle Lake District

Runways
01/19 3,077ft / 938m
07/25 6,027ft / 1,837m

A small airport which has never developed any significant traffic, although it is set to receive a number of new scheduled routes from Stobart Air in the near future. Carlisle has two runways and a small central terminal and hangar area. It is mostly used by light aircraft for training, along with the occasional biz jet and military helicopter visitors. You can see all parked aircraft from the access road and car park, but can on occasion be granted airside access if you ask.

The access road passes the Solway Aviation Museum next to the airport. It has a collection of historic military jet aircraft including a complete Vulcan bomber. Open weekends and public holidays from March to October www.solway-aviation-museum.co.uk

Public Transport: Bus #BR1 passes the airport entrance, linking it to central Carlisle.

Coventry

Runways
05/23 6,586ft / 2,008m

Despite many attempts, Coventry has never really made it as an airport for passenger flights. However it has always served some interest to the enthusiast as a home for preserved, vintage and stored aircraft. For many years the fleet of vintage Douglas airliners of Air Atlantique were based here, operating a mix of charter work and pleasure flights. The Classic Air Force operated a number of historic aircraft until the end of 2015 when most were dispersed to a partner organisation at Newquay Airport.

Coventry has a number of stored BAe ATP aircraft on the south side of the runway, and to the north is the DC-6 Diner, set inside a former Air Atlantique Douglas DC-6.

The passenger terminal was demolished recently, so most activity takes place on the western extreme of the airport, where cargo flights park and operate nightly. The northern portion of the airport is home to flying clubs and the Midland Air Museum, which has a nice collection of vintage civil and military aircraft. The museum opens daily www.midlandairmuseum.co.uk.

Rowley Road runs along the northern boundary of the airport, passing the museum. Follow it west until you come to Coventry Road. Turn left along it, passing through Bagington village. Pass the end of the runway and turn left onto a small road running parallel to the airport fence. From here you can see most aircraft on the airfield, and the runway.

Public Transport: Bus #539 links Coventry railway station with Bagington village. From there it's a 10 minute walk to either the museum or the spotting location.

Robin Hood Doncaster Sheffield

Runways
02/20 9,491ft / 2,893m

Hub For: Flybe, Thomson Airways

Formerly RAF Finningley, "Robin Hood" Doncaster Sheffield airport opened on the site in 2005 following the closure of Sheffield City Airport. The plan was to take advantage of the low-cost boom and offer an alternative for residents of the two nearby cities to airports at Leeds Bradford and Manchester. The airport has a very long runway, with a modern passenger terminal and parking apron to the west. North of this area, the former RAF hangars have been given new uses; one is home to a Cessna Citation service centre, which always has a few interesting aircraft visiting. Another is operated by the Vulcan Experience, which is the final home of XH558 – the last flying Vulcan. The organisation has recently acquired an English Electric Canberra to restore to flight, and if you visit the hangar you'll find part of a Boeing 727 fuselage and other aircraft inside.

Airline flights are operated by Thomson Airways, Flybe and Wizz Air, along with various seasonal charters. Often of interest are ad-hoc cargo flights which arrive in many different forms, from turboprops to Boeing 777s and Antonov 124s a number of times per week.

From the passenger terminal, drive or walk north past the hangars to reach the Vulcan Experience. Further along from here you can see aircraft parked at the Citation centre.

For general spotting and photography of movements, head out of the airport from the terminal, turn left onto Hurst Lane, and then left onto the A638. Turn left again onto High Common Lane, and first left at the roundabout onto Old Bawtry Road (postcode DN9 3BY). There are areas to park, and areas of higher ground.

Public Transport: Bus #588 passes the airport entrance and follows the route to the end of Old Bawtry Lane.

Durham Tees Valley

Runways
05/23 7,516ft / 2,291m

Situated to the east of Darlington and the west of Middlesbrough, Stockton-on-Tees, Yarm etc. Durham is some 20 miles to the north. The former RAF Middleton St George was known as Teesside Airport until 2004, and is quieter than it used to be. KLM Cityhopper and Eastern Airways provide daily scheduled flights, with some summer charter services. The airport is a popular base for GA flights and is a base for Cobham with its Dassault Falcon 20 fleet.

Most aircraft can be seen by driving or walking the road behind the hangars. Photography is possible from the railway station bridge beyond the flying clubs, or the layby off the A67 near the end of runway 23.

On the south east side of the airfield is a fire training ground with a complete Trident 3B and wrecks of a Viscount, ATR42 and Shorts 330. It is visibe from the railway station bridge.

Public Transport: Arriva bus #12 links the airport with Darlington.

Duxford

Runways

06L/24R 2,887ft / 880m
06R/24L 4,931ft / 1,503m

One of the principal aviation attractions in the UK. Duxford is a former wartime airfield of historic significance. Today it is home to the Imperial War Museum's main aviation collection, including that of the American Air Museum. It can take hours to work your way around the incredible collection of preserved aircraft from all major conflicts and civil eras, including a Concorde prototype.

Duxford is an active airfield for light aircraft and pleasure flights, and throughout the year it hosts some of the best air displays in the country, often with aircraft not seen at other shows.

Open daily from 10am (except Christmas bank holidays).
Visit www.iwm.org.uk for more information.

Public Transport: Bus #132 from Cambridge runs to Duxford on Sundays. There are also free buses from the city on air show days.

East Midlands

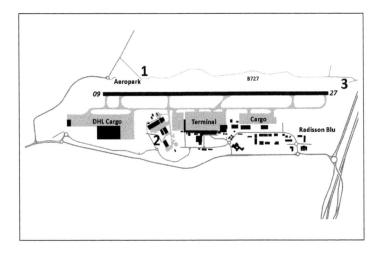

Runways

09/27 9,491ft / 2,893m

Hub For: bmi regional, DHL, Jet2, Ryanair, Thomas Cook Airlines, Thomson Airways, West Atlantic, UPS

East Midlands is probably the UK's most notable cargo airport. It successfully transitioned from a quiet regional airport by developing as a hub for cargo airlines such as DHL and UPS. These now serve the airport daily alongside their partners, such as West Atlantic, Star Air and Jet2. This is not to belittle the airport as a passenger base, with airlines such as Ryanair, Jet2, Thomas Cook, bmi regional and Thomson all offering a decent number of services.

Cargo flights operate mostly at night between 2100-0200 from Sunday to Friday. During the daytime you will only likely see a few DHL aircraft parked up, although there are usually more evident on Saturdays. UPS and Star Air aircraft usually park on the eastern cargo ramp, whilst all others use the large, dedicated DHL ramp at the western extreme of the airport.

Often unusual aircraft are visiting the paint hangars near spotting location 2 (see below), and look out for Boeing 727 fuselage now used as a fire trainer on the north side of the runway (formerly TC-ALB).

SPOTTING LOCATIONS

1. Castle Donington Crash Gate

Most spotters congregate at the crash gate on the northern side of the airfield as it is an accepted place to spot and offers the best views of all movements. To reach the gate, head to the village of Castle Donington. Close to the Aeropark museum, there's a pub with a small road next to it (Diseworth Road, postcode DE74 2PS). This road leads to the crash gate. You can see the passenger terminal and DHL apron, and all runway movements. It is good for photography through holes in the fence and once aircraft are above the fence line. You can also wander along the path which extends along the airport's northern boundary from here.

2. Hangar Area

From the airport's long stay car parks and access roads near DHL, you can drive to an area among the hangars which will yield any aircraft receiving maintenance, as well as some executive and light aircraft. You can photograph them through the fence, but don't stay too long in this area. Head for Dakota Road (postcode DE74 2TL).

3. Runway 27 Crash Gate

Another crash gate near the end of runway 27 is a good place to park up and watch aircraft movements. If you prefer to photograph with the sun behind you a trail heads off around the perimeter fence from here to the south side of the runway threshold where good shots of aircraft landing and lining up can be taken. The northern perimeter track also extends from this crash gate, eventually reaching location 1. Head for Ashby Road postcode DE74 2DJ.

East Midlands Aeropark is a compact outdoor museum of aviation exhibits, including a Nimrod, Argosy and Vulcan, and has good views of runway movements. Opens Thursday, Saturday and Sunday in summer, and Sundays only in winter www.eastmidlandsaeropark.org

HOTELS

Radisson Blu East Midlands

Pegasus Business Park, Herald Way, East Midlands Airport DE74 2TZ | +44 1509 67055 | www.radissonblu.co.uk

A recent addition. Many rooms overlook the threshold of runway 27 and parts of the eastern cargo ramp. You can see most movements, and photograph aircraft arriving/departing with a 300mm lens.

Public Transport: East Midlands Airport is linked to Derby, Leicester, Loughborough and Nottingham (and their railway stations) via bus services. Bus #155 from the passenger terminal also stops next to the Aeropark and spotting location 1 in Castle Donington.

Exeter

Runways

08/26 6,811ft / 2,076m

Hub For: Flybe

A modest regional airport in South West England serving the local population. It is primarily a base for regional carrier Flybe, which has its headquarters here, and sees various seasonal services throughout the year and nightly West Atlantic cargo flights.

The passenger terminal and Flybe's large hangar and apron occupy the southern boundary of the airport, with the east-west runway alongside. Further north of the runway former taxiways and the disused cross runway are usually home to a few stored airliners awaiting their next assignments.

There are no official viewing areas at Exeter any more. You can get views across the runway and terminal apron from long stay car park P3, but it is through a fence so photography is no good. Additional, car park P4 is situated alongside the Flybe apron, so you can see anything parked there.

Glimpses of anything stored on the north side are possible from the B3174 London Road as it heads north. It's easier if you find somewhere to park and then walk alongside the road.

Public Transport: Bus #56 links Exeter Airport with the city centre throughout the day.

Farnborough

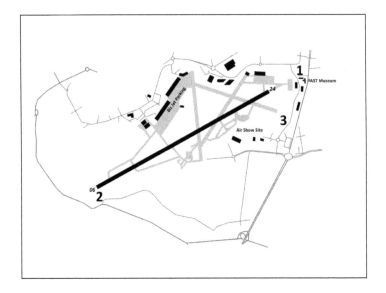

Runways

06/24 8,005ft / 2,440m

Most famous for its biennial air show, Farnborough has been the cradle for aviation development and testing in Britain for a long time. The airport is now a busy hub for biz jets bringing their owners to London and the South East, making it particularly attractive to enthusiasts.

The airport site is encroached upon by housing and the nearby town centre. Its main runway separates the two sides to the airport, with the control tower, FBOs and main parking aprons along the northern side. The southern side is reserved for the air show events, when large pavilions are erected and parking aprons designated for visiting aircraft.

SPOTTING LOCATIONs

1. Rae Road/FAST Museum

The cul-de-sac alongside the FAST Museum, Rae Road (postcode GU14 6XE) is more or less in line with runway 24. You can look along its length, and approaching aircraft will pass very low overhead. Walk a little along the main road to get a good vantage point, or read off (with strong binoculars) aircraft parked up on the north side.

2. Eelmore Bridge

At the 06 end of the runway is a distinctive iron bridge off the main A323 Fleet Road. It is technically on Laffan's Road (postcode GU11 2HL) and has a small area for parking. This location has great views of aircraft arriving and departing runway 06, and of departures off 24. You can see aircraft parked on some of the ramps, but not all.

3. Queen's Gate Road

When the air show is not on, Queen's Gate Road (postcode GU14 6GF) is a good route to follow (preferably park the car and walk along it) as it offers views across the runway to the various parking aprons on the north side.

Farnborough Air Sciences Trust (FAST) Museum is dedicated to the aviation history of Farnborough and its involvement in the development of aircraft and associated technology. It has some interesting displays and a number of aircraft outside. Open weekends and public holidays from 10am to 4pm. Visit www.airsciences.org.uk

Public Transport: From Farnborough Central Station, you can take bus #42 which passes the FAST Museum and Queen's Gate Road.

Gloucestershire

Runways
04/22 3,241ft / 988m
04G/22G 997ft / 304m
09/27 4,695ft / 1,431m
18/36 2,621ft / 799m

Gloucestershire Airport has gained something of a reputation in recent years as a centre for general aviation following a concerted effort by its management to carve a niche. After years following elusive scheduled services, the former wartime training base now only has daily links to the Isle of Man with Citywing, but is instead a hive of activity for light aircraft. It is also common to see biz jets present, especially with on-site training for these types.

The Aviator café is probably the best place for views. It serves food and drink and has outdoor seating with views over the airfield, flying clubs and runway 27 threshold, which is great for photographs. You can find it next to the airport entrance, off Bamfurlong Lane (postcode GL51 6SR).

Driving or walking further along the access road should yield more parked aircraft outside the many hangars.

Jet Age Museum

At the north west corner of the airport site, in Meteor Business Park (postcode GL2 9QL) is this small museum with a number of aircraft exhibits on display. Open weekends and public holidays from 10am to 4pm.

Public Transport: Bus #94 runs from Cheltenham to Gloucester, passing along the airport's northern perimeter and the Jet Age Museum. It is a short walk to The Aviator if you alight at Bamfurlong Industrial Park in Staverton Bridge.

Humberside

Runways
02/20 7,205ft / 2,196m
08/26 2,822ft / 860m

Hub For: Eastern Airways

Humberside is a small regional airport in North Lincolnshire, between Scunthorpe and Grimsby, and across the river from Hull. It is not busy, but sees daily scheduled services from KLM Cityhopper and Eastern Airways (which maintains its fleet here). Summer charters add to the mix, and there are plenty of helicopter flights to the North Sea oil rigs, and light aircraft movements from local training schools.

Views of anything parked near the passenger terminal or helicopter terminal can be obtained from the car parks and access roads.

A good location for watching arrivals on runway 21, where locals seem to prefer, is a small layby off the A18 along a road signposted for Grasby and Caistor. You can see across the runway to the parking ramps, and a little further along see part of a BAC 1-11 fuselage (G-AVMP) used for fire training near the smaller cross runway. This location is a 15 minute walk from the terminal.

Public Transport: The Humber Flyer bus service links the airport to both Hull and Grimsby.

Kemble Cotswold

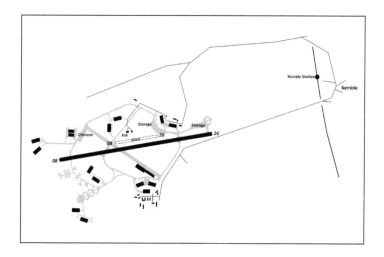

Runways
08/26 6,561ft / 2,009m
08G/26G 1,837ft / 560m

Whilst Kemble, known now as Cotswold Airport, is a busy GA airfield with a nice restaurant to visit, most enthusiasts will be drawn here for the ever changing landscape of airliners in long-term storage and being scrapped. On site companies such as ASI continually bring new types in from all over the world, particularly Airbus and Boeing airliners, and park them on the various ramps before they work their way to the scrapper.

Also in site are Chevron and Lufthansa Technik which provide aircraft maintenance, seeing many Avro RJ and BAe 146 types pass through.

Resident preserved and training aircraft include a Royal Air Force Bristol Britannia, VFW-614 and Boeing 737-300, and a couple of Hawker Hunter jets.

The A429 leading out of Kemble village passes the fence line where some store airliners can be read off. Then, back in the village follow signs for the airport and work your way from the entrance to the AV8 restaurant and control tower, where you will see other stored aircraft from different vantage points.

Public Transport: There is a railway station in Kemble village, but no public transport to the airport itself so you would need to walk around 3 miles.

Lasham

Runways

09/27 5,896ft / 1,797m

This small airfield in Hampshire has a long association with aircraft storage and maintenance. For many years it was the home to Dan-Air London's maintenance division. Whilst this has quietened down in recent years there is still a presence of older airliners in-between roles or at the end of their life most of the time. Lasham is also a busy gliding base.

Most enthusiasts pop by to catch a glimpse and hopefully a photograph of stored airliners. It's not possible to see all aircraft from one locations. The best locations to see them are from the crash gate at the northern end Lasham village (head past the Royal Oak pub, postcode GU34 5SL). From here you can see some of the stored airliners (look out for the derelict Boeing 727s in the trees on your left).

Another good location is the café of the Lasham Gliding Society, off The Avenue (postcode GU34 5SS) which runs parallel to the runway. You can see the many gliders and have views across to the hangars and stored airliners.

Leeds Bradford

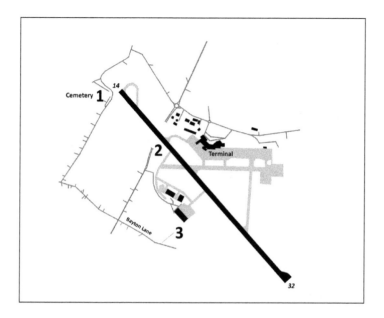

Runways
14/32 7,382ft / 2,250m

Hub For: Jet2, Monarch, Ryanair

Leeds Bradford has grown in stature in recent years and is now a base airport for Jet2, Monarch and Ryanair. Other airlines with daily or regular services include Aer Lingus Regional, Aurigny, British Airways, Eastern Airways, Flybe, KLM Cityhopper and Thomson Airways.

The airport has one runway, with former cross runways now acting as taxiways. The passenger terminal is on the north side of the runway, whilst to the south are maintenance hangars and the complex use for flight training by Multiflight. Spotting opportunities landside are limited around the terminal.

SPOTTING LOCATIONS

1. Cemetery

Walking to the north west you'll see the road tunnel which passes underneath the runway on your left. Continue over the roundabout, then left at the T-junction. You'll come to a cemetery which is used by local spotters which is great for runway 14 operations.

2. Runway Overlook

On the south side of the airport (head through the runway tunnel) there is an area overlooking the runway immediately on your left after the tunnel on higher ground.

3. Waste Ground

Alternatively, continue to a crossroads after leaving the tunnel and turn left onto Bayton Lane. A little further on your left is an area of waste ground overlooking parts of the airport and runway.

Public Transport: Bus #757 passes under the runway tunnel as it heads to and from the airport. It's possible to walk from the south side of the tunnel to any of the spotting locations in less than 20 minutes.

Liverpool John Lennon

Runways
09/27 7,497ft / 2,285m

Hub For: easyJet, Ryanair

Despite living in the shadow of the much larger Manchester Airport some 30 miles away, Liverpool has still managed to carve a successful operation from its substantial catchment area across the North West and North Wales. The airport's focus is on low-cost and leisure flights, and regional flights across the Irish Sea.

The airport is a hub for easyJet and Ryanair. Other carriers include Aer Lingus Regional, Blue Air, CSA Czech Airlines, Flybe, Thomson Airways, Vueling and Wizz Air. The airport usually sees a number of unusual football charters every year. To the north of the present airport on the old Speke Airport site the historic original Art Deco terminal is now a Crowne Plaza hotel, with a small collection of historic airliners being preserved outside including a Bristol Britannia and Jetstream 41.

Liverpool's modern terminal offers views once through departures, but is fairly restrictive for those without a ticket. For the best location head east from the terminal on Dunlop Road, which becomes Hale Road, then turn right onto Dungeon Lane. There are places to park, and you will see aircraft on the GA apron and using runway 27. Photographs are possible.

Public Transport: Bus #89 from the airport passes the end of Dungeon Lane and the GA hangar every 20 minutes.

Manchester

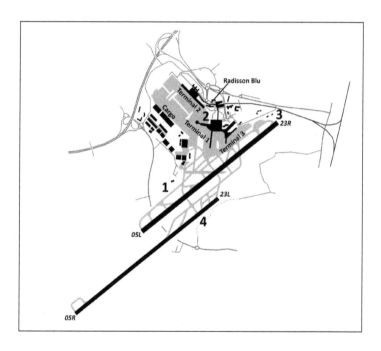

Runways
05L/23R 10,000ft / 3,048m
05R/23L 10,007ft / 3,050m

Hub For: easyJet, Flybe, Jet2, Monarch, Ryanair, Thomas Cook Airlines, Thomson Airways

Manchester is one of the favourite airports in the UK for aviation enthusiasts thanks to its excellent viewing facilities and fairly varied mix of movements. The airport can be busy at certain times of the day, particularly in the summer months.

Manchester is one of the UK's most important airports and has long been popular with both charter and scheduled carriers. The north of England gateway is the third busiest airport in the country, after Heathrow and Gatwick in the London area. Although traditionally the domain of charter airlines, it has now become very busy with low cost airlines.

Whilst long haul flights at Manchester have come and gone, today it enjoys a number of links to destinations further afield through American Airlines, Delta, Emirates, Etihad, PIA, Qatar Airways, United and Virgin Atlantic. Emirates flies two of its three daily services using its Airbus A380 super jumbo. A number of cargo carriers also provide daily widebody aircraft for added interest, including Lufthansa Cargo.

Manchester Airport has three passenger terminals and a cargo terminal, along with an extensive maintenance area comprising large hangars and bays. The airport has two parallel runways.

SPOTTING LOCATIONS

1. Runway Visitor Park

What must be the best official viewing facility in the UK is located at Manchester. The Runway Visitor Park was built on the north side of Runway 05L/23R to replace facilities lost when the new runway was built and rooftop terrace closed. Purpose-built mounds raise the enthusiast over the height of the fence to allow photography of aircraft on the runway and taxiway. Also at the RVP is an aviation shop, café, toilets and various preserved airliners – some of which are open to the public. These include a DC-10 section, British Airways Concorde, Trident, Nimrod and Avro RJX. The park is open daily (except 25/26 December) from 8am till dusk (4pm in winter, 6pm in spring/autumn, 8pm in summer). The entrance fee is for cars, depending on how long you stay. Those on foot/bike enter free. www.runwayvisitorpark.co.uk

2. Multi-Storey Car Park

For many years the top level of the Short Stay Car Park outside Terminal 1 was one of the main spotting locations. It is still a popular stop off as it offers fantastic views over the cargo and maintenance ramps, as well as Terminal 2, parts of Terminal 1, and the runways in the distance. Spotting and photography are still good from the car park's open roof. This is a good spot to log what's not visible from the Runway Visitor Park, but parking charges can prohibit extended stays.

3. Airport Hotel Pub

Located at the threshold of Runway 23R. The beer garden here backs up to the taxiway and holding point for the runway and is ideal for landing shots. A very pleasant summer afternoon can be held here, with food and refreshments on tap. This is a 15 minute walk from terminals 1/3.

4. South Side

A favourite for the photographers is a spot on the south side of the airport, alongside runway 23L/05R. Instead of turning into the Runway Visitor Park, continue along Wilmslow Road (A538) and through the tunnels underneath the runways. Immediately afterwards, turn left at the roundabout onto Altrincham Road. Park here, or in the adjacent hotel car park, then follow the footpath towards the perimeter fence. The sun is in a good position and the airliners are very close!

HOTELS

Radisson Blu Hotel

Chicago Avenue, Manchester M90 3RA |
+44 (0) 161 490 5000 | www.radissonsas.com

The best hotel for spotting at Manchester. Located behind Terminal 2, rooms on high floors overlook the aprons and the runways in the distance. The restaurant also offers this view. Some good opportunities for photographs with a long lens. The hotel is rarely cheap.

Public Transport: Manchester Airport has its own railway station with local and national links. Buses also link the airport to central Manchester, and can be used to reach the Runway Visitor Park (bus #200) and the south side viewing area (bus #88 from the RVP).

Newcastle

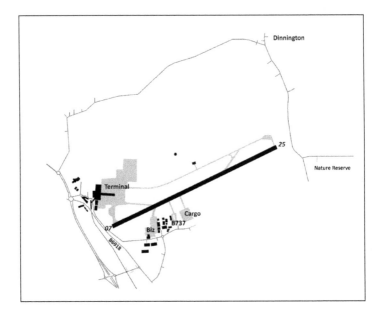

Runways

07/25 7,641ft / 2,329m

Hub For: easyJet, Jet2, Thomas Cook Airlines, Thomson Airways

A growing regional airport in the North East. Newcastle is a popular hub for holiday and low-cost flights, as a base for easyJet and Jet2. Other airliner traffic of note include a daily Emirates Boeing 777, various Ryanair routes, Aer Lingus Regional, British Airways, Flybe, CityJet, Eurowings, KLM, Thomson Airways, Thomas Cook Airlines and Eastern Airways.

The passenger terminal is on the north side of the single runway, on the eastern boundary of the airport. On the south side is a small cargo ramp (Jet2 737, FedEX ATR and West Atlantic ATPs most evenings), and a ramp for GA and executive aircraft. A local training college is also home to some airframes including a former WestJet Boeing 737-200 easily visible outside.

The best opportunities for spotting are at either end of the runway as no views exist landside in the terminal any more. At the southern end (runway 07), walk from the terminal along the B6918 until you reach the approach lights and metal gate leads to a small field where photographs can be taken.

At the opposite end (runway 25) the car park of a nature reserve is perfect for parking up to watch and photograph arrivals from the east. You can't see any aircraft on the ground from here, however, so it is only good for 25 arrivals. This is a short drive from the terminal, via Dinnington. Head for Coach Lane (postcode NE13 7BP).

Public Transport: Newcastle Airport is easy to reach on the Tyne & Wear Metro. The nature reserve spot is on bus route #44 from Regent Centre Metro stop.

Newquay

Runways
12/30 9,003ft / 2,744m

This moderately busy regional airport and former RAF base is situated in the south west corner of Britain. Flights are operated to UK and Ireland destinations, with some seasonal holiday flights, by Aer Lingus Regional, Flybe and Ryanair. There is also a popular link to the Scilly Isles.

The passenger terminal is on the north side of the runway, whilst the south side and former military section of the airfield is being turned over to other business uses. The Cornwall Aviation Heritage Centre is an interesting attraction for enthusiasts. In recent years some airliner scrapping has taken place at Newquay.

Spotting is possible in the car park next to the passenger terminal. It is also possible to get views through the fence from near the control tower on the former RAF site.

Additionally, a layby near the end of runway 30 is also a good spot to pull in and watch any aircraft landing in that direction.

The **Cornwall Aviation Heritage Centre** has a collection of historic aircraft which can be powered up, and even offers scenic flights. Aircraft include a VC-10, BAC One-Eleven, Harrier, Hunters, Sea Devon and Varsity. Open Sunday to Friday, www.cornwallaviationhc.co.uk

Public Transport: Bus #56 links central Newquay with the airport passenger terminal.

North Weald

Runways
02/20 6,171ft / 1,881m
13/31 2,703ft / 827m

An interesting general aviation airfield near Epping, between London and Chelmsford. North Weald Airfield was an important Battle of Britain station and many of the remaining buildings on the site are listed. Today it is a busy gateway for private aircraft flights, and is home to a number of vintage aircraft. A number of flying events are organised each year.

The Squadron is the club house for North Weald Flying Services. It is accessed by requesting permission from the gate, which then involves driving around the taxiway. Beware of parked and taxiing aircraft! From here you can see most of the aircraft and any movements. Access is via Hurricane Way (postcode CM16 6AA).

Public Transport: Buses #381, #419 and #420 all link Epping with North Weald Airfield

Norwich

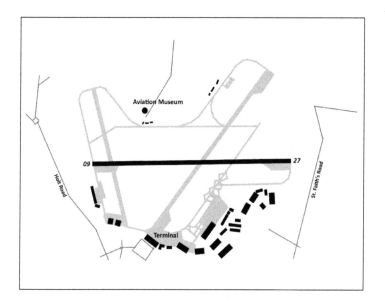

Runways
09/27 6,040ft / 1,841m

Norwich Airport handles around half a million passengers per year, mostly on scheduled flights by bmi regional, Eastern Airways, Flybe and KLM Cityhopper. In the summer months holiday flights are operated by a number of operators. Offshore helicopters and some FBOs also operate from Norwich.

The airport is also home to a KLM Engineering base, so sees the Cityhopper fleet passing through regularly, and other airliners come in for painting and maintenance fairly frequently.

A stock of stored airliners are sometimes resident, which in the past have included some interesting airframes.

The car park and roads around the terminal are usually sufficient for seeing any aircraft parked on the aprons.

There are small laybys on the roads at either end of the runway for good views and photographic opportunities of approaching aircraft. For runway 09 head to Holt Road (postcode NR10 3DD), and for runway 27 heard to St. Faith's Road (postcode NR12 7BH).

The **City of Norwich Aviation Museum** occupies a site on the northern boundary of the airport. It has a number of historic aircraft, including both a Fokker F-27 and Handley Page Herald of Air UK, which have significance to the airport. The museum is open daily in the summer and Wednesday, Saturday, Sunday and public holidays in the winter. See www.cnam.org.uk

Public Transport: Park and Ride buses link Norwich Airport with the city centre and train station. Local buses also pass nearby.

Oxford Kidlington

Runways
01/19 5,092ft / 1,552m
11/29 2,493ft / 760m

London Oxford Airport, to give its full branding, is a fairly small airport 7 miles north of the city, next to the town of Kidlington. It no longer has passenger services, but is kept busy with executive aircraft movements and as the home of CAE Oxford Aviation Academy – the largest pilot training organisation of its kind in Europe. Its fleet of single- and twin-engine aircraft are on the go most days.

Langford Lane (postcode OX5 1RY) runs past the southern end of the main runway. There is a small layby to park in, and good views across the airport where you'll see most of the parked aircraft easily.

There are views of other parked aircraft and helicopters if you explore the access roads, but part of the site is behind a security gate.

Public Transport: Bus #2C links central Oxford with the airport, via Kidlington.

Retford Gamston Airport

Runways

03/21 5,522ft / 1,683m
15/33 2,764ft / 842m

Although it has no passenger service, Retford Gamston is a busy general aviation site and sees occasional biz jet visitors. There are numerous flying clubs based here, and Diamond Executive Aircraft have a base. It is often possible to gain permission to walk airside along the line of hangars to log and photograph aircraft, and the café has a good reputation and decent views.

Southampton

Runways

02/20 5,653ft / 1,723m

Hub For: Flybe

One of Flybe's busiest bases, Southampton Airport is fairly busy but limited by its runway length. Nevertheless a number of summer services are also operated by the likes of Thomson Airways and Volotea. Additional scheduled services are flown by Aer Lingus Regional, Aurigny, bmi regional and KLM Cityhopper.

The passenger terminal and FBOs are on the western side of the runway.

There are two good places to watch aircraft at Southampton, but security are known to move people on from both. The first is the short stay car park alongside the terminal and railway station. Although looking through a fence, you have a good view of part of the parking apron and photography is possible.

The second viewpoint is reached by walking north along Mitchell Way towards the long stay parking. Past the hangars there is a raised area on your right which looks over the fence line to the runway and is great for photography.

Public Transport: Southampton Airport has its own railway station outside the terminal, linked to the South West Trains network.

London

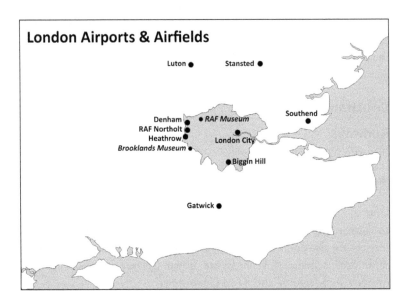

Deserving its own section, London is the busiest airspace in the United Kingdom with the highest density of major airports and significant airfields. The map here shows the location of those listed below in relation to the city itself; transport links to all are fairly good, and the aircraft traffic is also noteworthy to the enthusiast.

Additional aviation attractions in and around London include the excellent Brooklands Museum at Weybridge, and the Royal Air Force Museum at Hendon, both also labelled on the area map.

Denham

Runways

06/24 2,543ft / 775m
12/30 1,791ft / 546m

Denham Aerodrome is just inside the M25 London Orbital motorway, close to where the M40 intersects. It is 13 miles north of Heathrow Airport. Denham has a concrete and a grass runway and is a busy general aviation airfield for London. Light aircraft and helicopters make up most movements, with the occasional biz jet or prop.

The airfield is split into north and south sections, with Tilehouse Lane linking them. The north side is home to The Pilot Centre flying school, who are known to allow airside access for logging and photography if you have a hi-viz vest. The south side has a parking area alongside the fence and a restaurant with views.

Public Transport: Denham Aerodrome is a 30 minute walk from the nearby Denham Station and bus routes.

London Biggin Hill

Runways

03/21 5,971ft / 1,820m
11/29 2,585ft / 788m

Biggin Hill was a wartime base famous for its involvement in the Battle of Britain. Located near Bromley, some 14 miles south of central London, today it acts as a gateway for biz jets and general aviation traffic. It currently has a ban on scheduled services, preventing it from entering the competitive market for flights to London, but nevertheless sees aircraft up to the Airbus A320 and Boeing 737 size, albeit as executive transports.

Various FBOs are located at Biggin Hill, using hangars and aprons along the western and southern boundaries of the airport, alongside its L-shaped runway pattern. The passenger terminal is on the western side, off the A233. On the eastern side are hangars and aprons generally used by light aircraft and companies involved in the restoration of heritage aircraft.

The new Lookout Coffee Shop opened in 2015 offering a place to enjoy a drink whilst watching aircraft movements at Biggin Hill. You can find it on Maitland View (postcode TN16 3BN). From here you will see most movements, particularly on the main runway and nearby parking areas.

A security barrier prevents you from exploring any deeper within the airport complex without a good reason. Alternatively you can try outside the passenger terminal for a quick view of parked aircraft.

Public Transport: Bus #320 links Biggin Hill with Bromley railway station, which has links to London.

London City

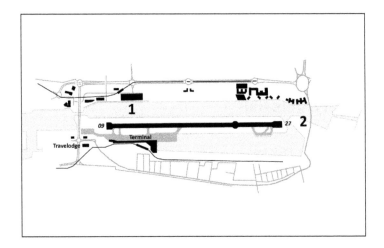

Runways
09/27 4,948ft / 1,508m

Hub For: BA CityFlyer, CityJet

At the heart of London's Docklands, built on a former dock, is the tiny London City Airport. Despite its size and short runway, this is a busy hub and even has daily transatlantic services using British Airways' dedicated Airbus A318 fleet. The airport is a hub for BA Cityflyer and CityJet, and is served from Europe's capitals and business destinations by Alitalia CityLiner, Flybe, Lufthansa Regional, Luxair, SkyWork Airlines and Swiss International Air Lines. Given the restrictions on runway length and the steep approach angle owing to nearby skyscrapers the airport's movements are mostly limited to regional jets and turboprops.

The airport has recently been cleared for an expansion of its terminal, parking apron and taxiways which will likely see more flights introduced. At present the airport is busiest early in the morning and late in the evening. It closes for flights for a 24 hour period between 1pm Saturday and 1pm Sunday.

The small terminal building and apron are on the south side of the runway, with a dedicated ramp for biz jets to the east.

SPOTTING LOCATIONS

1. Opposite Dock

Opposite the airport there is a walkway running the length of the runway with great views. From here you will see every movement, and be able to read off aircraft parked at the terminal. Some parked biz jets are a little awkward to read from here, however. Photography is also great from this spot with a 300mm lens. To get here head for Royal Albert Way, off the A1020, or walk 20 minutes across the Connaught Bridge from the terminal; it is also the Royal Albert stop on the DLR. The University of East London is here, and there is ample parking space.

2. Runway 27

When heading north on the A112, take a right turn into the industrial estate, and then turn left and follow the road under the A112 to a small car park. This spot is very close to the end of Runway 27, so you get a good view down the runway which is perfect for photography. It's a 25 minute walk from the terminal.

HOTELS

London City Airport Travelodge

Hartmann Road, Silvertown, London E16 2BZ |
0871 984 6333 | www.travelodge.co.uk

A short distance from the terminal and on the main access road. Higher rooms facing north have a view over the end of runway 09 and the biz jet ramp. The best ones are 503 to 509. You shouldn't miss too many movements from here. Please note that these are family rooms, so you'll need to request one when booking.

Public Transport: The airport is served by buses and the Docklands Light Railway which links to the London Underground and mainline train stations.

London Gatwick

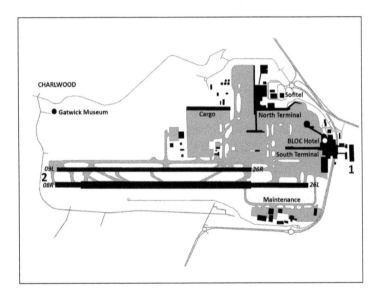

Runways
08L/26R 8,415ft / 2,565m
08R/26L 10,879ft / 3,316m

Hub For: British Airways, easyJet, Monarch, Norwegian Air Shuttle/ Long Haul, Thomas Cook Airlines, Thomson Airways, Virgin Atlantic

Gatwick, London's second largest airport, is situated to the south of the city next to the town of Crawley. Whilst it is the world's busiest single-runway airport operation, you'll note that a second runway does exist, albeit acting as a taxiway except when the main strip is out of operation. Thus Gatwick can appear a crowded and busy place during peak hours.

British Airways retains a healthy presence at Gatwick, operating short, medium and long haul services with a dedicated fleet that will not usually be seen on an average visit to Heathrow. Additionally many leisure and low-cost airlines operate from here, with a few airlines not seen elsewhere including Iraqi Airways, Med-View Airline, Meridiana and Tianjin Airlines. Cathay Pacific have also chosen Gatwick as one of its first Airbus A350 destinations.

Gatwick has two terminals – North and South. The North Terminal is home to British Airways and easyJet, and has a unique passenger bridge over the taxiway with airliners passing below.

Sadly Gatwick lost its excellent viewing terrace on the South Terminal in favour of expansion in the early 2000s. This left Gatwick with no official viewing facilities, and it has since proved a very frustrating airport for the enthusiast. For those with a flight ticket, the sports bar in the South Terminal is an excellent place to watch the movements, as is a suitable room at the BLOC Hotel.

SPOTTING LOCATIONS

1. Multi-Storey Car Park

The top level of the Multi-Storey car park at the southern end of the South Terminal is a nice spot for logging aircraft on short finals to Runway 26L. Facing into the sun is not ideal, however. Signs at this location indicate that spotters are not welcome to loiter. A similar view exists from the platforms of the railway station.

2. Runway 08R

Following Charlwood Road and Lowfield Heath Road (postcode RH11 0QB) around the end of Runway 08R leads to a crash gate which is close to aircraft lining up on the runway. It is possible to photograph or log aircraft, including those on short final to land. This is the most popular spot for spotters these days, however parking is not allowed near the gate itself so you will need to walk to reach it.

HOTELS

BLOC Hotel

South Terminal Gatwick Airport, RH6 0NP |
+44 20 3051 0101 | www.blochotels.com

Situated atop the South Terminal in the former administration building, the BLOC Hotel is a great place to spot if you have a room facing the airport. It has similar views to the old viewing terrace. Depending on the room you will usually have a view of both terminals and part of the runway.

Sofitel London Gatwick Airport

North Terminal, Gatwick Airport RH6 0PH |
+44 1293 567070 | www.sofitel.com

Smart hotel situated at the North Terminal, and linked via monorail from the South Terminal. Rooms on the higher floors facing the airport, such as 898, have unrivalled views of aircraft movements to both terminals.

Public Transport: Gatwick Airport has a rail station outside the South Terminal with fast train services to central London and Brighton. Catch bus #26 from the South Terminal (also stops near the North Terminal) to Charlwood, which is next to the Gatwick Aviation Museum, and a ten minute walk from spotting location 2.

The **Gatwick Aviation Museum** at Charlwood, close to the end of runway 08L/R at Gatwick houses a nice little collection of military jets and historic aircraft. It is open Friday, Saturday, Sunday 10am to 4.30pm, www.gatwick-aviation-museum.co.uk.

London Heathrow

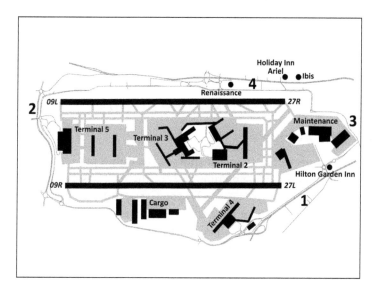

Runways

09L/27R 12,802ft / 3,902m
09R/27L 12,008ft / 3,660m

Hub for: British Airways, Virgin Atlantic

Heathrow is Europe's busiest airport and at times is very overcrowded. A decision over a new runway in south east England has been held up many times, leaving Heathrow to struggle with capacity and ambitions for growth. Nevertheless, the variety of airlines operating here can be mouth-watering to the enthusiast, coming from all corners of the globe. It is the operating and maintenance base for both British Airways and Virgin Atlantic, and features as a destination for many world carriers.

Heathrow has two parallel runways, 09L/27R and 09R/27L. Patterns of runway assignment between landing and departing switch at 3pm every day. In the central area is Terminal 2, which opened in 2014 for Star Alliance carriers, Terminal 3 which is the oldest and due for redevelopment, and the site of the former Terminal 1 which is currently being redeveloped as an extension to Terminal 2. Terminal 5, for British Airways and Iberia flights, is to the west, whilst Terminal

4 is located to the south east of the runways. Cargo aircraft park to the south, and maintenance areas are to the east.

Heathrow sees large numbers of Airbus A380s and Boeing 787 Dreamliners amongst the airlines flying in. Cargo carriers are quite limited, with relatively few movements compared to other European hubs.

SPOTTING LOCATIONS

1. Myrtle Avenue

This is one of the most popular spots at Heathrow, but is only useful when aircraft are landing on runway 27L. The spot gets its name from a small residential street close to Hatton Cross, with a grass area at the end. Spotters congregate on this area to log and photograph aircraft as they pass low overhead. There is very limited parking, so it's best to walk from Hatton Cross Tube Station.

2. Runway 09L Approach

Stanwell Moor Road runs the length of the western perimeter of the airport, behind Terminal 5. At its northern end there is often space to park up at the side of the road. Aircraft pass low overhead on approach to runway 09L, and are also visible approaching 09R (but it's hard to photograph those).

3. Runway 27R Approach

A walk along the Eastern Perimeter Road can help you find a good spot to watch arrivals on 27R. Security patrols regularly monitor this area and ask spotters to stay a few metres from the fence. You can take good photographs here of arrivals, but can't see any other parts of the airport.

4. Academy/Renaissance Hotel

Even if you're not staying in the Renaissance Hotel, the car park next to it was formerly the home of the Heathrow Visitors Centre. Today it is the Heathrow Academy and has an enthusiast's shop. From here you can get good views of all movements on the northern runway (09L/27R) from a small grandstand. It is not the best place for photographs. This spot is located off the Northern Perimeter Road.

HOTELS

Renaissance London Heathrow

140 Bath Road, Hounslow TW6 2AQ |
+44 20 88 97 63 63 | www.marriott.com

This is one of the best spotting hotels in the world, if you request a room overlooking the airport. All movements on the northern runway can be read off and photographed easily. Movements around the terminals are easy to spot. Those using SBS can continue to spot throughout the night. Although this hotel is not the cheapest at Heathrow, the quality of spotting makes up for it and it offers special spotter packages through its website.

Hilton Garden Inn London Heathrow

Eastern Perimeter Rd, Hounslow, TW6 2SQ |
+44 20 8266 4664 | www.hilton.com

Formerly the Jury's Inn. There are rooms which face south, overlooking aircraft on short final to runway 27L, or north/west which look out over part of the airport and the northerly runway. Choose which you'd prefer and make a request.

Holiday Inn London Heathrow Ariel

118 Bath Road, Harlington, Hayes UB3 5AJ |
+44 20 89 90 00 00 | www.holidayinn.com

Another good spotting hotel at Heathrow. Even-numbered rooms between 270 and 284 have the best views of aircraft using the northern runway and terminal areas. Photography is possible. The hotel is more affordable than the Renaissance.

Ibis London Heathrow

112 Bath Rd, Hayes, London UB3 5AL |
+44 20 8759 4888 | www.ibis.com

A little further east than the Ariel. Odd-numbered rooms on the top floor are great for watching and photographing arrivals on runway 27R. You can't see much on the ground, but it is a short walk to the perimeter road.

Public Transport: Naturally Heathrow is well served by public transport links from London and surrounding areas, plus the national bus network. You can reach all terminals and nearby Hatton Cross (good for spotting location 1) on the London Underground Piccadilly line. The airport is also linked to Paddington Station by the Heathrow Express train.

Buses running around the perimeter roads and between terminals are free to use. You can reach spotting locations 3 and 4 using bus #285 from the central terminal area, or bus #423 from Terminal 5.

London Luton

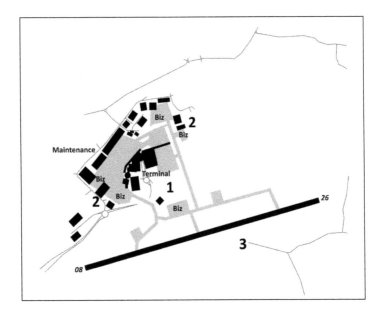

Runways
08/26 7,087ft / 2,162m

Hub For: easyJet, Monarch, Ryanair, Thomson Airways, Wizz Air

Luton is London's fourth largest airport, and is situated some 30 miles north off the main M1 motorway. Today the airport is a busy gateway for low cost carriers and holiday charter airlines. It is the home base of easyJet, Thomson Airways and Monarch Airlines. Ryanair and Wizz Air also have a heavy presence. A number of cargo airliners pass through each day.

Luton is perhaps best known amongst enthusiasts for the large variety of business jets which pass through on a regular basis. The airport has many ramps and hangars dedicated to this traffic, which can be a little difficult to navigate around and see everything, but there are always plenty to see including some from far off places.

Luton has a cramped and confusing central area which includes the terminals, car parks, roads, hotels and administration buildings. You will see signs around this area discouraging spotters from stopping. If you have some time to spend here, it's best to spend it at the viewing area alongside the runway. Otherwise a quick stop to log through the fence should be fine.

SPOTTING LOCATIONS

1. Central Area

Driving around the access roads to the hangars, cargo centre and other parts of the central complex will offer glimpses of many business jets and other aircraft parked around the various aprons. Signs discourage spotters from parking in these areas, so make only quick stops to log what you can see. You can park at the Holiday Inn for the nearer ramps, and you can usually afford a brief stop outside the Long Term car park (follow the road as far as you can) to log the biz jets parked alongside it.

2. Crash Gate

Head away from the terminal area towards the M1. Turn right at the second roundabout and then right again towards Wheathamstead. After a couple of miles, turn left at a crossroads, under a railway bridge and up the hill. Turn left at the next junction and keep right. Turn left at the houses, and park alongside the road when it reaches the fence. Keep the crash gate clear at all times! Views of aircraft using the runway are good from here, and photography is possible.

HOTEL

Holiday Inn Express Luton Airport

2 Percival Way, Luton LU2 9GP |
+44 1582 589100 | www.hiexpress.com

Rooms facing the airport are all great for logging aircraft on the runway and some taxiways, and also have plenty of opportunities for good photographs.

Public Transport: Buses #99, #757, #A and National Express coaches all link central Luton with the airport, which is a short distance. The free bus to the Long Term Car Park is a good option for reaching the spotting locations there.

London Southend

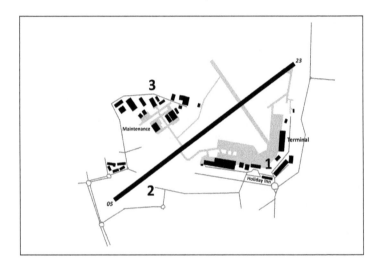

Runways
05/23 6,089ft / 1,856m

Hub For: easyJet

Rebranded like many periphery airports around the capital to take advantage of passenger traffic from the significance of serving London. Southend is in fact over 40 miles to the east in Essex, but has up to eight trains per hour linking it to Liverpool Street Station in around 50 minutes.

Southend Airport has long been an enthusiast favourite because of the interesting mix of aircraft usually present, and the memories of early independent carriers which would ply their trade here. In recent years, under new management, Southend has focussed more on passenger services having attracted the likes of easyJet and Flybe to boost the number of passengers passing through its new terminal building and runway extension. However, the companies focusing on aircraft maintenance and storage still exist and exploring the service roads usually uncovers a few interesting airframes.

SPOTTING LOCATIONS

1. Car Parks

The southern part of the passenger terminal car parks have views across the ramp and of some of the stored airliners, as does the access road if you walk along it.

2. Runway Viewing Area

When the runway was extended the main road passing behind it was truncated, leaving small sections on both the south and north sides which have views onto the runway and small areas to park up.

3. Aviation Way

This road leads behind the various hangars and warehouses on the northern side of the airport. It is where most of the stored aircraft and those receiving maintenance can be found, and a drive along here uncovers various vantage points. Postcode SS2 6UN.

HOTELS

Holiday Inn Southend Airport

*77 Eastwoodbury Cres, Southend-on-Sea SS2 6XG |
+44 1702 543001 | www.holidayinn.com*

This hotel's location is perfectly suited for in-room spotting. All rooms on the north side of the building (including Standard, Executive, and King Superior rooms) face towards the runway and terminal ramp. The rooftop restaurant and bar also has panoramic views.

Public Transport: Train services link the passenger terminal with London Liverpool Street Station. Bus #9 from the passenger terminal routes past the end of the runway and spotting location 2.

London Stansted

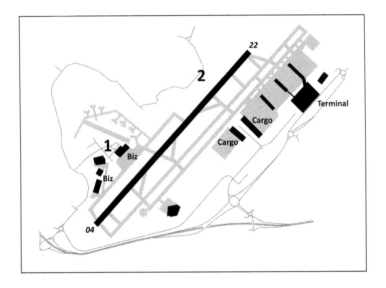

Runways
04/22 10,003ft / 3,049m

Hub For: easyJet, FedEx Express, Ryanair

Stansted is a fairly busy airport 30 miles north east of London. It saw dramatic growth in the mid-1990s when the impressive single terminal building, designed by Sir Norman Foster, was opened to replace the facilities on the original site which had, until then, been a largely forgotten regional airport.

The airport had started life as a bomber base and maintenance depot in the Second World War. The potential for passenger operations were realised when the British Airports Authority (BAA) took over in 1966.

When low-cost airlines Ryanair, Go and Buzz wanted cheaper access to London, Stansted was chosen and it quickly grew to handle the demand. Go was quickly swallowed by easyJet, and Buzz by Ryanair, leaving these two airlines as the main operators. Today number of other low-cost airlines also have a large presence at Stansted, including Air Berlin. Many charter and cargo airlines can also be found operating through Stansted on a daily basis.

Stansted has a single runway. On the north side extensive aprons and hangars for executive aircraft movements can be found, along with a resident L1011 TriStar is used as a trainer.

The passenger terminal has three concourses of gates which are not visible from the rest of the terminal. Further to the west are two areas of cargo aprons and warehouses where the many daily flights park up. These include carriers such as Asiana, Cargolux, China Southern, Ethiopian Airlines, Korean Air Cargo, Qatar Airways, Silk Way, Turkish Airlines Cargo and UPS Airlines.

SPOTTING LOCATIONS

1. Old Terminal Area

On the opposite side of the airport close to the runway 04 end is the old terminal area, now used for maintenance, executive jets, and aircraft storage. There is a long-term resident L1011 TriStar here, and on any day there are likely to be some exotic business jets present. When exiting the M11 towards the airport, follow signs for Long Stay car parks and Business Park, following Round Coppice Road. Turn right onto First Avenue (postcode CM24 1RY) into the Business Park and look for places to quickly log what you can see without blocking any roads. Security have been known to move people on from this area.

2. Opposite Runway

Drive back and turn right to continue along Bury Lodge Lane. In the tiny village of Burton End turn left onto Belmer Road (use postcode CM24 8UL). After half a mile find a place to park by the side of the road, and then walk through the paths in the trees to find an official viewing area alongside the fence, opposite the runway. You have distant views of the passenger and cargo terminals, but all runway movements are easy to see and photograph.

HOTELS

Radisson Blu London Stansted Airport

Waltham Close, Stansted Airport, Essex CM24 1PP |
+44 1279 661012 | www.radissonblue.co.uk

A very smart, modern hotel at Stansted with prices at the higher end. Some higher rooms facing the airport have views over the Ryanair pier and Runway 23 threshold. The hotel is only a few metres from the Terminal.

Public Transport: The passenger terminal has a railway station linking to London, and buses arrive from many places. It's not possible to get to either of the spotting locations via public transport.

RAF Northolt

Runways
07/25 5,535ft / 1,687m

Northolt is an active Royal Air Force base situated around 6 miles north of London Heathrow Airport. It is of interest to the civil enthusiast still due to its regular use by executive aircraft and the home of the Royal Flight aircraft.

Because of its sensitive nature and military use, Northolt is not the easiest of airports to spot at and extra care should be taken not to draw attention to yourself.

The airport has one main runway, with disused cross runways still evident. To the south is the main parking apron for biz jets, whilst the military area is to the north. Most movements occur on weekdays.

West End Road/A4180 (postcode HA4 6NG) passes the end of runway 25. Just past the petrol station the hedge disappears and you have a view down the runway. Park somewhere nearby and walk to this spot and you'll be able to see most of the parked aircraft, albeit at a good distance.

The busy A40 passes the southern side of the airport. If you park up and walk along here you may be able to see some of the parked biz jets over the fence.

Public Transport: Ruislip Gardens is the nearest London Underground station, and South Ruislip is the nearest mainline train station to RAF Northolt. Buses run past the base frequently.

Northern Ireland

Belfast City George Best Airport

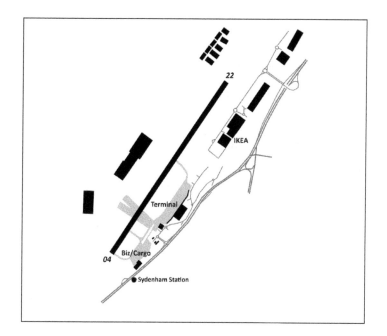

Runways
04/22 6,001ft / 1,829m

Hub For: Flybe

Renamed after the local footballing legend, the former Belfast Harbour airport is a small facility located within easy reach of the city centre and nearby docklands and Titanic attractions.

Traffic consists mostly of commuter flights to other UK cities, however Aer Lingus provides some seasonal holiday flights. Other carriers include British Airways, Brussels Airlines, Citywing and KLM

Cityhopper. The limited runway length and parking space has restricted much further growth.

The passenger terminal is on the eastern side of the runway, close to the A2 motorway. Cargo and executive aircraft park on a separate ramp further south. Walking through the car parks from the terminal should yield views of aircraft parked here.

To the north of the terminal, alongside the runway, is a large IKEA store with a multi-storey car park which can be used for logging and photographing during store opening hours providing you don't draw too much attention. It is accessed from the next exit of the A2 after the airport (follow signposts for Holywood Exchange).

Public Transport: Sydenham railway station is close to the airport terminal, linked from central Belfast.

Belfast International

Runways
07/25 9,121ft / 2,780m
17/35 6,204ft / 1,891m

Hub For: easyJet, Jet2

Around 11 miles north west of Belfast is the main international airport for the city and Northern Ireland. It shares the site with a military helicopter base on the site of the former RAF Aldergrove which closed in 2008 and occupied the southern part of the airport.

The majority of passenger operations are by easyJet, Jet2, Ryanair, Thomson Airways and Thomas Cook. Scheduled services by mainline carriers tend to use Belfast City, however transatlantic links with United Airlines are Virgin Atlantic do use this airport.

Belfast International is also a busy cargo hub with a dedicated cargo ramp and hangars to the west of the passenger terminal. Daily flights are operated by ASL, DHL, Star Air and Swiftair freighters. It's easy to see these aircraft by walking left out of the passenger terminal.

The airport has two runways running at right angles to each other. The aprons of the former RAF base are largely unused now. A Trident 2 airliner (G-AVFE) can be seen in the long grass at the western extremity of the airport, used as a fire trainer.

A small parking area to the east of the airport offers fairly decent opportunities to photograph aircraft approaching runway 25 about half a mile before touchdown. To reach it, drive west from the airport on Airport Road and turn right onto Drennans Road, then left at the crossroads with the church. The car park is a few hundred metres on your left (postcode BT29 4EN).

Public Transport: Translink's Airport Express 300 links Belfast International with the city centre and onwards to elsewhere in Northern Ireland.

City of Derry

Runways

08/26 6,460ft / 1,969m

A quiet airport in the north west of Northern Ireland around 7 miles east of Londonderry/Derry. It has a single active runway with two disused cross runways. The passenger terminal and parking apron is to the south of the runway, with flights provided by Ryanair.

You can try following Clooney Road from the airport entrance, then turning right onto Airport Road (postcode BT47 3PZ) to reach the flying club where the runway and any parked aircraft can be seen.

Public Transport: Ulsterbus links the airport terminal with the city centre.

Scotland

Aberdeen

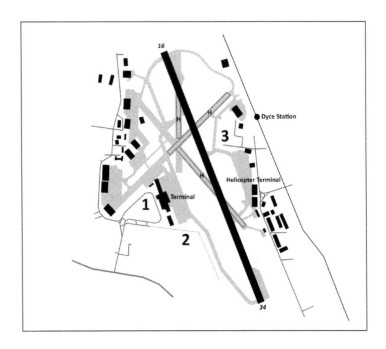

Runways

16/34 6,407ft / 1,953m

Hub For: bmi regional, Eastern Airways, Flybe

Aberdeen is a busy airport in north east Scotland which is a hub of activity surrounding the offshore oil industry, with much of its traffic made up from helicopters ferrying workers to and from rigs.

Airline flights to Aberdeen are often related to this also, with links to all regional airports across the UK, to Norway, and many European financial centres. A link has also been opened up recently to Reykjavik with Air Iceland DHC-8 Q400s. Some seasonal flights exist to holiday destinations, and cargo flights are operated by Loganair, Ben Air and West Atlantic.

The passenger terminal is to the west of the runway, with a dedicated helicopter terminal on the east side. Bristow and other helicopter operators have maintenance bases to the north of the passenger terminal

SPOTTING LOCATIONS

1. Terminal Car Park

The top of the car park outside the passenger terminal is good for quick views of aircraft taxiing and parked on some of the ramps, including the helicopters. Photography is possible, but you may be moved on from this location.

2. Viewing Shelter

At the southern corner of the terminal building is a shelter and some benches with views over part of the airliner parking apron and the runway beyond. You can see all movements from here and take some good photographs through the fence.

There is no parking here, so you'll need to walk from the terminal car park along the track/disused road next to the car rental building.

3. Cordyce View

On the eastern side of the airport Cordyce View (postcode AB21 7DS) is a residential street which runs to a crash gate. Opposite the houses is the fence next to the helicopter terminal and executive aircraft apron, which you can photograph through. The crash gate also looks out onto the runway, and has a small space for parking cars. Alternatively you can walk 5 minutes from nearby Dyce railway station.

HOTELS

Holiday Inn Express

3, International Ave, Dyce, Aberdeen AB21 0BE |
+44 1224 608300 | www.hiexpress.com

This is a new hotel built to the south of the terminal, close to other hotels but it seems it has the best views of all of them. Ask for a room facing the runway for views of aircraft movements and helicopter operations.

Public Transport: Bus #727 links the airport to the city, whilst Dyce railway station links the city to the helicopter terminal. Bus #80 travels between the passenger terminal and helicopter terminal.

Barra

Runways
07/25 2,621ft / 799m
11/29 2,231ft / 680m
15/33 2,776ft / 846m

Probably the most unusual airport in the British Isles. Barra's three runways are all on the beach. A daily Flybe/Loganair Twin Otter link to Glasgow is governed by the times of the tides, with aircraft parking up next to the sand dunes and small terminal building. Good views of aircraft movements can be had from the area north of the terminal.

Benbecula

Runways
606/24 6,023ft / 1,836m
17/35 4,003ft / 1,220m

A rural airport with two runways on the island of the same name in the Outer Hebrides. Daily services to Glasgow and Stornway with Flybe/ Loganair Saab 340s and Twin Otters. The passenger terminal and parking apron are at the southern side of the airport, with good views through the fence. The access road also has views of the runway.

Camplbeltown

Runways

11/29 5,741ft / 1,750m

Despite its rural island location, Campbeltown has the longest runway in Scotland, giving up its former role as a NATO base. Today it is sustained by a public service flight link to Glasgow with Flybe/Loganair DHC-6 Twin Otters.

Public Transport: Bus #443 links the airport to Cambeltown.

Dundee

Runways

09/27 4,593ft / 1,400m

A small regional airport on the banks of the Firth of Tay, which has had mixed fortunes with commercial services. Flybe and Loganair provide a few daily scheduled turboprop flights, alongside a busy general aviation community. The passenger terminal and GA parking are at the eastern end of the airport. Views are possible from the flying club car parks.

Public Transport: Bus #5 and #9 pass close to the airport from the city centre and railway station.

Edinburgh

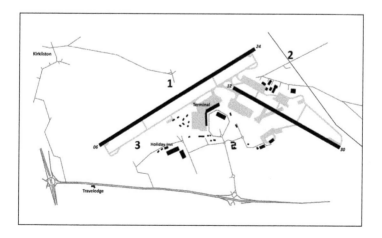

Runways

06/24 8,386ft / 2,556m
12/30 5,896ft / 1,797m

Hub For: easyJet, Flybe, Jet2, Ryanair

Scotland's busiest airport. Edinburgh Airport has grown significantly in recent years, managing to pull off expansion in full service, low cost and cargo services. Key operators of interest to the enthusiast include Air Canada Rouge, American Airlines, Atlantic Airways, Delta, Etihad Airways, Norwegian Air Shuttle, Qatar Airways, Transavia France, Turkish Airlines, United Airlines and Vueling.

The passenger terminal occupies a central position on the airport site, with the main runway to the north. The secondary runway and cargo base are to the east.

SPOTTING LOCATIONS

1. River Almond Bridge Gate

On the northern perimeter of the airport at roughly the mid-point of the main runway is a crash gate just off a bridge over the River Almond, which is popular with local spotters. There is room for a few cars to park and you can see and photograph all movements on the runway. To reach the location head to the village of Kirkliston (beyond the airport, off the M9 motorway). At the village centre head east on Main Street (postcode EH29 9AD) for a mile or so.

2. Lennymuir Railway Bridge

Turnhouse Road (postcode EH12 0AZ) runs to the cargo site on the east of the airport. You can't get any good views of these aircraft, but if you park your car and walk along Lennymuir (EH12 0AP) there is a railway bridge with good photographic opportunities of aircraft approaching runway 24.

3. Western Car Parks

A 15 minute walk west of the passenger terminal is a large open air car park which fronts the perimeter fence alongside the taxiway and runway 06 threshold. Head for the Holiday Inn Express hotel and continue past it.

HOTELS

Travelodge Edinburgh Airport

Ratho Park, Glasgow Rd, Edinburgh EH28 8PP |
0871 984 6340 | www.travelodge.com

Ask for a room overlooking the A8/Glasgow Road. These face the threshold of runway 06, giving you views of most movements. It would be beneficial to be on the top floor as trees outside the hotel can obscure the view.

Public Transport: Trams now link Edinburgh Airport with the city centre, alongside buses.

Glasgow International

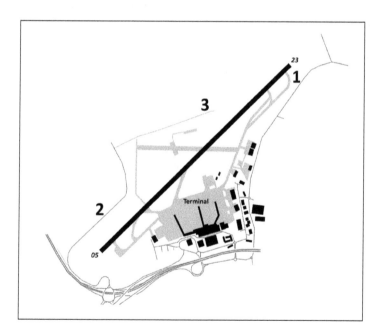

Runways

05/23 8,743ft / 2,665m

Hub For: easyJet, Flybe, Loganair, Thomas Cook Airlines, Thomson Airways

Glasgow's main airport handled close to 9 million passengers last year. It is a busy gateway to Scotland, with many domestic, European and long haul links. Many long haul routes are seasonal, such as those by Air Canada Rouge, Air Transat, American Airlines, Delta, Virgin Atlantic and WestJet. However, Emirates and United Airlines provide year-round service, and there are many low-cost and scheduled services to keep spotters interested.

The passenger terminal sits to the south of the runway and has three piers. There are no real views from the terminal unless you have a flight ticket, so it's best to head to one of the locations around the perimeter.

SPOTTING LOCATIONS

1. Abbotsinch Road & Runway 23

From the terminal head under the M8 and then turn left onto Abbotsinch Road. This passes the Loganair hangars, cargo area and FBOs on the eastern side, so it's worth exploring before continuing along the road until you find a layby on the left which looks out to the threshold of runway 23. Aircraft can be photographed landing but you may wish to walk back along the road to find a better view of aircraft on the ground.

2. Barnsford Road

From the terminal head west for Barnsford Road/A726 (postcode PA3 2TQ) which loops around the end of runway 05. A crash gate adjacent to the threshold is popular, but there's only space for one car to park. A footpath along the road helps you find a good spot to view and photograph through the fence.

3. Walkinshaw Road

Continuing along Barnsford Road you'll come to a small lane called Walkinshaw Road on your right (postcode PA4 9LP) which runs along the northern perimeter to a farm and crash gate. Do not block the road or crash gate, or park on the farm's land. You have a good view across the airport and runway here, with most of the terminal in view and decent photography opportunities through the fence.

Public Transport: Bus #500 links the airport with Glasgow city centre, and #757 with Paisley.

Glasgow Prestwick

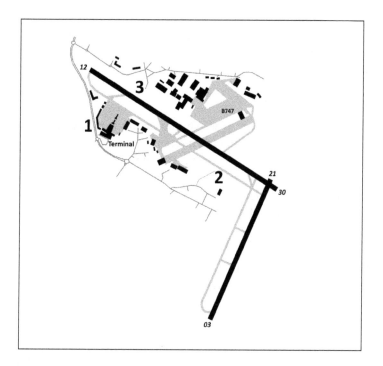

Runways
12/30 9,797ft / 2,986m
03/21 6,250ft / 1,905m

Hub For: Cargolux, Ryanair

Prestwick in Ayrshire is no longer the stopover point for aircraft heading across the Atlantic, but it does still see some interesting traffic – particularly military and cargo movements. Passenger flights are now limited to Ryanair, however freight services by the likes of Air France Cargo, Cargolux and Volga-Dnepr are common. Various airlines use the airport for line training.

Prestwick has two runways at right angles. The passenger terminal and cargo apron are at the western side, with hangars and maintenance areas on the north side; a Boeing 747 training airframe (N852FT) can be seen here.

SPOTTING LOCATIONS

1. Terminal Viewing Gallery

You can view and photograph airliners on the ground from the spectator's galley upstairs in the passenger terminal. Photographs are through glass.

2. Spotting Mound

A popular unofficial place to watch movements is a mound and area of waste ground close to the intersection of the two runways. It has views across to the apron used by biz jets and some cargo aircraft, and excellent views of the runway. To reach the location head east from the terminal along the A79, Shawfarm Road, and then left onto Shaw Road (postcode KA9 2LN). The track to the waste ground is on your left.

3. Monkton Crash Gate

On the northern side of the airport in the village of Monkton there is a crash gate along Main Street (postcode KA9 2QL) with room to park. Views through the fence are of aircraft lining up and approaching runway 12, albeit mostly into the sun.

Public Transport: A railway station outside the terminal gives swift access to central Glasgow, Ayr, Kilmarnock and Paisley. Bus #4 links the airport with Monkton, with a short walk to location 3.

Inverness

Runways
05/23 6,191ft / 1,887m
12/30 2,297ft / 700m

Hub For: Loganair

The capital of the Highlands. Inverness Airport is a few miles east of the city at Dalcross and is a hub for flights around the country and to the Orkney and Shetland islands.

Loganair is the main operator, with cargo flights and passenger flights through its franchise with Flybe. Other carriers include British Airways, easyJet and KLM Cityhopper.

A popular spotting location can be found just inside the airport entrance (postcode IV2 7JB). At the first roundabout, turn right down a dead end which leads to a crash gate. Spotters often park here, and you have a good view of arrivals on runway 05 and can see any aircraft parked at the terminal.

The **Highland Aviation Museum** (postcode IV2 7XB) is hidden among the industrial estate behind the terminal and car parks. It has a nice little collection of aircraft and cockpits, including a Nimrod, Herald and Victor. Open weekends and public holidays.

Public Transport: Bus routes link Inverness Airport with both Nain and Inverness city centre.

Islay

Runways
08/26 2,083ft / 635m
13/31 5,069ft / 1,545m

In the southern part of the island around 5 miles north of Port Ellen. Regular scheduled services by Flybe/Loganair with Saab 340s to Glasgow, and other communities with Hebridean Air Services Islanders. Any parked aircraft can be seen from the passenger terminal.

Public Transport: Bus #451 links the airport with Port Ellen.

Kirkwall

Runways
09/27 4,685ft / 1,428m
14/32 2,231ft / 680m

The principal gateway to the Orkney Islands at the main town. It is served by Flybe/Loganair services to Scotland's main airports, and local Loganair services to remote airports across the Orkneys and Shetlands. Aircraft can be seen from around the terminal area, or the separate GA area to the west.

Public Transport: Bus #4 runs between the airport and the town/harbour.

Oban

Runways

01/19 4,147ft / 1,264m

A scenic small airport on the west coast of Scotland and around 6 miles north of the town which has rail and ferry links. The airport is only served by local Hebridean Air Services links using Islander aircraft, but is a popular spot for visiting GA aircraft.

You can see parked aircraft easily from the passenger terminal. There is also a crash gate looking out onto the southern runway boundary on Lora View (postcode PA37 1RR).

Public Transport: Buses #005 and #918 both link Oban with the airport terminal.

Perth

Runways

03/21 2,799ft / 853m
09/27 1,998ft / 609m
15/33 2,034ft / 620m

Perth is not a commercial airport, but is one of the busiest general aviation airfields in Scotland. It is three miles north east of the city and has a number of flight training schools based. A Handley Page Jetstream I (G-NFLC) is used as a ground trainer.

If you bring a hi-viz vest and ask at the tower or flying schools you are likely to be permitted access airside to see aircraft on the ground and in the hangars.

Public Transport: Bus #57 links Perth Airport with Perth and Scone.

Stornoway

Runways
06/24 3,281ft / 1,000m
18/36 7,595ft / 2,315m

One of the busier airports in the Scottish islands. Stornoway is served by Eastern Airways and Flybe/Loganair on flights around the country. It also handles mail flights and has a small helicopter base for the Coastguard.

The passenger terminal is on the eastern side of the airport and aircraft can easily be seen through the fence.

Public Transport: The #W5 bus service links Stornoway town centre and ferry port with the airport.

Sumburgh

Runways
09/27 4,921ft / 1,500m
15/33 4,678ft / 1,426m

The main airport for the Shetland Islands, situated at the southern tip and some distance from the main town at Lerwick, which has its own tiny airport.

Sumburg has two main runways and a small helicopter runway. The main 09/27 strip has a road running across the 09 threshold with barriers to stop traffic when movements occur. Movements are mainly by Flybe/Loganair and Bristow Helicopters.

The passenger and helicopter terminal is on the airport's eastern side, meaning the access road runs a circuitous journey around the airport perimeter, giving ample views of the runways and parked aircraft. Walls around the car park unfortunately limit views of parked aircraft, but the gravel parking area on the entrance road near the Sumburgh Airport Memorial has good views of any movements.

Public Transport: A bus service links Sumburgh Airport with Lerwick.

Tiree

Runways

05/23 4,829ft / 1,472m
11/29 2,621ft / 799m
17/35 2,598ft / 792m

A former RAF training base on the island of Tiree. It has a small terminal building and parking apron on the west side of the airport, with daily Flybe/Loganair flights to Glasgow. Aircraft parked on the apron are visible from the terminal area.

Wick John O'Groats

Runways

13/31 5,988ft / 1,825m

Wick is a small airport that has recently been rebranded to attract travellers to the nearby John O'Groats at the north east corner of the British mainland. The airport is nevertheless quite quiet, served by Eastern Airways and Flybe/Loganair turboprops a few times per day from a small terminal which has views of any aircraft parked up.

The hangars and business park limit views from the entrance road

Wales

Aberporth

Runways

08/26 4,124ft / 1,257m

Close to the Pembroke Coast National Park, Aberporth is at present no more than a general aviation airfield. But its rebranding as West Wales Airport is part of a plan to attract scheduled airline services, particularly on domestic flights within Wales. The airport also hopes to become a centre for unmanned drone operations and development.

The airport's hangars and administration buildings are on the north side of the runway and you can see anything parked up by driving or walking around this area. The crash gate on the south side, where the recent runway extension truncated the road, is also a good viewing point providing you don't obstruct the gate.

Anglesey

Runways

01/19 5,377ft / 1,639m
08/26 4,200ft / 1,280m
14/32 7,513ft / 2,290m

Anglesey Airport occupies part of the RAF Valley base, which is an active training centre for Hawk aircraft. The airport's only service is a subsidised link to Cardiff operated at present by Citywing.

A large parking area alongside Minffordd Road (postcode LL65 3NA) at the entrance to the passenger terminal and base is a great place to watch movements. There is a Hawker Hunter gate guard alongside and a good view of the runway 19 approach and nearby parking aprons.

Public Transport: Bus #4 links the airfield with central Holyhead. It passes the spotting location mentioned above.

Cardiff

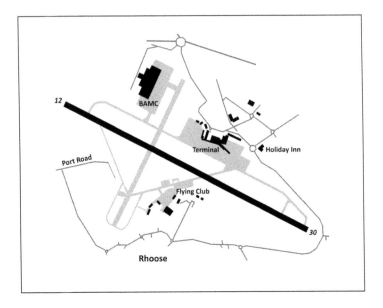

Runways

12/30 7,848ft / 2,392m

Hub For: Flybe, Thomson Airways

The busiest and largest airport in Wales, serving its capital on the south coast. Cardiff handles just over a million passengers per year, mostly on regional flights and holiday charters. The airport is home to the British Airways Maintenance Cardiff site, which occupies a large hangar and separate aircraft apron to the north west of the passenger terminal. Here the airline's long haul fleet are maintained, including Boeing 747, 767, 777 and 787 aircraft. This gives the airport an interesting mix of visiting aircraft, but it is nothing you won't see in abundance at Heathrow. Other carriers include Aer Lingus Regional, KLM Cityhopper and Vueling.

The south side of the runway is home to a Rhoose Flying Club and its Cambrian Flying Bar, which is an excellent viewing location with an outdoor balcony and views across to the runway and terminal. Reach it by following Porthkerry Road around the end of runway 30 and following signs (postcode CF62 3EQ).

Another popular viewing location is Port Road (postcode CF62 3BH), beyond the Highwayman Inn, which has a track running along the fenceline with views of the runway. You may need a ladder for photographs. Look out for the BAC One-Eleven fire trainer fuselage (G-AVMT) alongside the former cross runway nearby.

Public Transport: Cardiff Airport is linked to the city via the TrawsCymru T9 bus every 20 minutes. Bus #303 links the airport with Rhoose, with the Station Road stop a short walk from the flying club.

Chester Hawarden

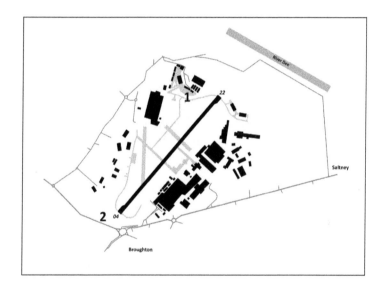

Runways
04/22 6,699ft / 2,042m

Hub For: Airbus

Built close to the English border and the city of Chester, Hawarden Airport is a Welsh airport heavily involved in the production of parts for Airbus aircraft. These are transported by A300 Beluga aircraft to the factories in Hamburg and Toulouse most days of the week.

Although no passenger services exist, airlines such as bmi regional often provide employee flights from Hawarden to Airbus sites in Bristol and Toulouse.

Hawarden is also a good place to catch biz jets either involved in Airbus activities, or visiting the on-site Marshall Aerospace servicing facility which looks after Beechcraft and Cessna types.

SPOTTING LOCATIONS

1. Chocks Away Diner

The Chocks Away Diner (www.chocksawaydiner.co.uk) at the general aviation area on the north side of the airfield is a good place to eat and watch aircraft movements. Open daily.

2. Runway 04 End

The B5125 Chester Road (head for postcode CH4 0NQ, St Mary's Way) runs past the end of runway 04 with a great view along its length. With a good pair of binoculars you'll see most parts of the airfield. You cannot park here, so find a place in nearby Broughton and walk a few minutes to find a good spot.

Public Transport: Bus #4 and #21 from central Chester to Hawarden pass along Chester Road on their way to the depot on the west side of the airport.

MOD St Athan

Runways
08/26 5,997ft / 1,828m

St Athan is a few miles west of Cardiff Airport. It is still an active Ministry of Defence site which has been heavily involved in Royal Air Force training in the past. The airfield is also one of the UK's main airliner storage and scrapping locations due to developments in recent years, which has brought it back to the enthusiast's attention.

All of the airfield's buildings, hangars and aprons are on the north side of the runway. Movements are few, but a drive around should uncover any stored airliners present. It is not wise to loiter too long due to the military presence.

From St Athan village, drive north along Cowbridge Road (postcode CF62 4LE). This passes the end of runway 08, but not much will be visible. Turn left into the base entrance when you see it, and follow this around the northern part of the airfield. You will have some views of the stored airliners through the fence on your left, so log them quickly without causing an obstruction. Further on some roads into the residential area on your left have limited views through the fence.

Public Transport: Bus #303 travels all the way from central Cardiff, via Cardiff Airport, to St Athan base, passing through the village and stopping close to the place to see the stored airliners.

Swansea

Runways
04/22 4,429ft / 1,350m
10/28 2,812ft / 857m

Efforts to bring commercial services to Swansea have never gone far, with the last flights ending in 2004. It is mainly used for general aviation, training and helicopter rescue flights, but it is hoped to develop the airport with new facilities to attract more aviation business. The car park outside the flying club is a good place to log any aircraft on the ground. It has views through the fence to the main runway.

Public Transport: Bus #118 from central Swansea passes Swansea Airport.

Channel Islands and Other Islands

Alderney

Runways

03G/21G 1,631ft / 597m
08/26 2,877ft / 877m
14G/32G 2,405ft / 733m

Hub For: Aurigny

A small airport on the tiny island of Alderney. Of its three runways in a triangle pattern, only 08/26 has a hard surface. The small terminal building is due to be replaced or upgraded, but the airport is unlikely to get any busier. Links to Guernsey and Southampton operated by Aurigny. You can usually see parked aircraft from the terminal, or from surrounding roads.

Bembridge, Isle of Wight

Runways

12/30 2,713ft / 827m

Bembridge is one of a few airfields on the Isle of Wight. It does not have any passenger services, but is popular among the GA community. It is of note as an assembly location for Cirrus aircraft, and the home of Britten-Norman whose aircraft are built elsewhere but sometimes present. You can log aircraft from outside the tower.

Public Transport: Bus #8 passes Bembridge Airport from both Newport and Bembridge.

Guernsey

Runways
09/27 5,194ft / 1,583m

Hub For: Aurigny

The second busiest of the Channel Islands. Guernsey is a hub for intra-island flights, with Aurigny based here. Other airlines of note are Blue Islands, Flybe, West Atlantic and Air Berlin which operates flights in the summer with DHC-8 Q400s. Biz jets are also common here.

The views in the terminal are usually sufficient for watching movements and logging airliners. You can also use the car park on the north side of the runway off La Villaze Road which has views across the airfield. If you don't have a car, it is a 25 minute walk from the terminal.

Guernsey has a number of wrecked aircraft on the fire dump north of the runway. Approaching the fire service may yield a visit.

Public Transport: CT Plus operates three different bus services to Guernsey Airport, one of which loops the island.

Isle of Man

Runways
03/21 4,117ft / 1,255m
08/26 6,923ft / 2,110m

Hub For: Citywing

Commonly known as Ronaldsway Airport. Situated at the southern end of the island between Castletown and Ballasalla. Most traffic is by regional turboprop aircraft from the likes of Aer Lingus Regional, Flybe and Citywing's LET 410s. easyJet and British Airways bring jet aircraft, but the runway lengths limit anything larger.

There is an area to view aircraft movements in the terminal which overlooks the parking ramp and runways beyond. Alternatively Derbyhaven is a small village on the coast to the south of the airport which has views across the airfield. Follow the A5 to Castletown and then Derbyhaven road east from the Promenade to reach the area. You can walk here in 30 minutes, but there is no public transport.

Isles of Scilly St. Mary's Airport

Runways

09/27 1,722ft / 525m

14/32 2,277ft / 694m

Hub For: Isles of Scilly Skybus

St. Mary's Airport is a small two-runway facility which handles flights by Isles of Scilly Skybus on most days to Lands End, Newquay and Exeter. Some GA aircraft are also based here. Aircraft can be seen from the terminal or by following High Cross Lane around the northern end of runway 14.

Jersey

Runways

08/26 5,597ft / 1,706m

Hub For: Flybe/Blue Islands, Flybe

The busiest of the Channel Island airports, surviving on a steady mix of scheduled traffic to both France and the British mainland, and a range of summer charters. Because links with Germany are still strong it is common to see summer flights from Air Berlin, Germanwings and Lufthansa. Principal carriers at Jersey are Aer Lingus Regional, Blue Islands, British Airways, easyJet and Flybe.

The large, modern terminal does not have any viewing areas unless airside. To the east the road passes the biz jet parking apron and reaches the grass GA parking area. You can see through the fence here, but at the Jersey Aero Club there is a balcony and café/restaurant which is perfect for watching aircraft movements.

If you have a car there are two positions on the northern perimeter where you can park and watch movements through the fence. The first is on La Route de l'Hermite just outside St. Peter's. The other is along Rue de l'Eglise heading west out of St. Peter's with a handy footpath to find the best spot.

Public Transport: Bus #15 links St. Helier to Jersey Airport.

Republic of Ireland

Cork

Runways

07/25 4,298ft / 1,310m
17/35 6,998ft / 2,133m

Hub For: Aer Lingus, Aer Lingus Regional, Ryanair

Less than 5 miles south of the city, Cork Airport is the Republic of Ireland's busier airports. It is a fairly small airport, with two runways crossing each other. The terminal is in the north east corner, alongside a small cargo terminal and apron. Light aircraft use a separate parking area linked to the southern end of the longest runway, 17/35.

Both main Irish carriers, Aer Lingus and Ryanair, maintain a heavy presence here with a mix of regional and leisure routes. Some other carriers offer seasonal links to Cork, but the variety is not extensive.

The top floor of the multi-storey car park next to the terminal is a good place to see aircraft on the ground and using the main runway.

You can also drive to the flying school by following R600 south (signposted Kinsale from the terminal access road) and turning into their car park. From here you can see any aircraft parked on their ramp, and also the main runway beyond.

Finally, a popular spot for watching aircraft movements particularly when arriving and departing on runway 35 is a layby at Lios Cross. Follow the R600 south and turn right onto the small road in Bowen's Cross. Follow this for a mile and you'll see the layby and airport.

Public Transport: Bus #226 links Cork Airport with the city centre every hour.

Donegal

Runways

03/21 4,908ft / 1,496m

A remote airport in the extreme North West of Ireland with a single runway between a beach and tidal area. The airport has a small parking apron and terminal at the southern end, with views from the car park and the road passing the southern end of the runway. The only airline movements are ATRs from Aer Lingus Regional, and regular helicopter services to offshore rigs.

Dublin

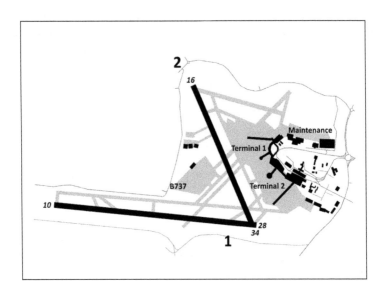

Runways

10/28 8,652ft / 2,637m
16/34 6,798ft / 2,072m

Hub For: Aer Lingus, Aer Lingus Regional, ASL Airlines, Ethiopian Airlines, Ryanair

When built in 1940, the terminal at Dublin's airport was considered to be the best in Europe and won architectural accolades for its designer.

Following the Second World War the number of services increased rapidly. Three hard runways were laid, and new hangars and other buildings built. A terminal extension could only cope a few years into the long-haul jet revolution, and in 1972 another new building was opened with a capacity of 1.6 million passengers per year. The current main runway 10/28 was opened in 1989.

The passenger terminal has required steady expansion, and in 2006 opened its new pier to alleviate pressure from Aer Lingus and Ryanair movements. Other carriers with a decent presence include British Airways, Ethiopian Airlines, Flybe and Thomson Airways. Long haul links are provided by Air Canada Rouge, American Airlines, Delta, Emirates, Etihad, United and WestJet.

Dublin has become one of the fastest growing European airports and the US pre-clearance facility has propelled the stature of Aer Lingus' transatlantic services, combined with connecting regional flights from across the UK and Europe.

Biz jets park on an apron at the northern side of the airport, which is difficult to see from the terminal or even aircraft windows. The cargo apron is opposite the passenger terminal, to the north of the main runway. Look out for a retired Ryanair Boeing 737-200 (EI-CJD) in the same area.

Sadly no official spotting facilities remain at Dublin, but a number of locations around the perimeter are popular.

SPOTTING LOCATIONS

1. Runway 10/28

Following the road away from the terminal, turn on to Old Airport Road, which follows the perimeter. You'll soon be alongside the main runway, and depending on the direction in use you can find raised spots at either end of the runway which give you an elevated position for photography. Many spotters congregate here. Photography is good, and most traffic will pass you eventually. Follow the road around for spots on the northern side of the runway. Buses #16 and #41 heading for Dublin will drop you ½ a mile from this location (Dardistown Cemetery). A car is recommended.

2. Runway 16

Following the perimeter road around will lead you past the fire station and to the threshold of Runway 16. Parking along the side of the road, you can take good photographs here. This runway is not used as much.

HOTELS

Radisson Blu Dublin Airport

Dublin Airport |
+353 1 844 6000 | *www.radissonblu.com*

Rooms facing the airport have a distant view of movements at Dublin. If aircraft are arriving on runway 28, or using the new international pier, you should see them. Too distant for photography.

Public Transport: Bus routes #16 and #41 link Dublin Airport with the city centre.

Dublin Weston

Runways
07/25 3,030ft / 1,381m

Weston is Dublin's second airport, located 9 miles west of the city. It is primarily a general aviation airport, but sees executive aircraft movements regularly. You can see most parked aircraft from the car park, or by using the restaurant in the flying school.

Public Transport: Bus #67 from central Dublin passes close to Weston. Alight at Cooldrinagh Lane and walk the last 15 minutes to the terminal.

Kerry

Runways
08/26 6,562ft / 2,000m

Kerry is a small airport in western Ireland served by Ryanair and Aer Lingus Regional on a few domestic and European routes. It is very quiet, with little general aviation or other services. The airport's runway replaced an earlier runway closer to the terminal which still exists but is disused.

Any aircraft parked outside the terminal can be seen from the car park

Public Transport: Buses link Kerry Airport with Tralee, Killarney and Limerick. There is a railway station in Tralee.

Shannon

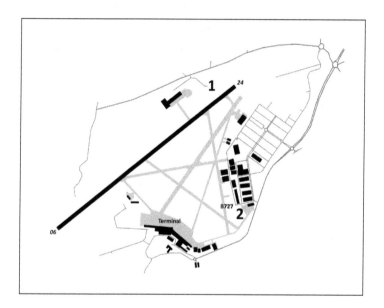

Runways

06/24 10,495ft / 3,199m

Hub For: Aer Lingus, Ryanair

No longer a regular transatlantic stop-off point for many airliners, Shannon still sees its fair share of traffic crossing the pond. In recent years British Airways has started using it as a staging post for its London City to New York Airbus A318 flight, and it still has seasonal links with American Airlines, Delta and United. Otherwise, traffic consists of summer charters, and European schedules by Aer Lingus and Ryanair. Cargo traffic is fairly busy with carriers such as ASL Airlines, Turkish Airlines Cargo and Star Air.

The passenger terminal occupies the southern side of the airport. Maintenance and storage areas are on the eastern and northern peripheries of the airport, with a main runway running south west to north east.

Often you'll see exotic aircraft at Shannon undergoing maintenance or painting, or in storage. There's also an old Iberia Boeing 727 (EC-CFA) used by the fire service, visible to the east of the terminal.

SPOTTING LOCATIONS

1. There is a public viewing area next to the Shannon Aerospace hangar on the northern perimeter of the airport, close to the runway 24 threshold. The majority of aircraft use this direction for landing, so you will see most movements. The fence is a little high for photographs unless you have a step ladder.

2. Exploring the Shannon Industrial Estate on the eastern side of the airport should give you views of some of the aircraft parked outside the maintenance hangars.

Public Transport: Buses #51, #343 and #398 all link Shannon Airport with central Limerick.

Waterford

Runways
03/21 4,700ft / 1,433m

A small regional airport which recently lost its scheduled services to the UK. At present the only operations here are light aircraft and ad-hoc charters. The car park outside the terminal is usually sufficient to see any aircraft parked up.

Aviation Museums & Collections

AeroVenture South Yorkshire Aircraft Museum

Dakota Way, Airbourne Road, Doncaster, DN4 7NW |
01302 761616 | *www.southyorkshireaircraftmuseum.org.uk*

A large collection of early aircraft, fast jets, helicopters and smaller civil airliners. Most inside large hangar, with some outside and in smaller buildings.

Open Tuesday-Sunday 10am-5pm (late March-late October), 10am-4pm (November-March). Adults £6, Seniors £5, Children £2.50, Family £13.50. Under 5s free.

Bournemouth Aviation Museum

Merritown Lane, Hurn, Christchurch, BH23 6BA |
01202 473141 | *www.aviation-museum.co.uk*

A compact collection of vintage jets, warbirds, airliners and helicopters, mostly just cockpit sections but some complete. Located next to Bournemouth Airport.

Open daily 10am-4pm (late March-late October), 10am-5pm (late October-late March). Adults £6, Children £3, Under 3s free.

Brooklands Museum

Brooklands Road, Weybridge, Surrey, KT13 0QN |
www.brooklandsmuseum.com

Occupying the historic Brooklands race circuit and former aircraft factory where many British types were built. Museum combines aircraft and automotive history. Impressive collection of airliners (VC-10s, Vanguard, Varsity, Viscounts, Concorde prototype) and wartime aircraft. Many are open to enter.

Open daily 10am-5pm (March-late October), 10am-4pm (November-February). Adults £12.50, Seniors £10, Children £6, Family £30, Under 5s free.

City of Norwich Aviation Museum

Old Norwich Road, Horsham St Faith, Norfolk, NR10 3JF |
01603 893080 | *www.cnam.org.uk*

Small museum on the north side of Norwich Airport. Has complete Nimrod, Vulcan, Herald, Fokker F-27, Lightning, Jaguar, Hunter, Meteor and other types.

Open Tuesday-Saturday 10am-5pm, Sunday & public holidays 12-5pm (April-October); Wednesday & Saturday 10am-4pm, Sunday 11am-3pm (November-March). Adults £4.50, Concession £4, Children £2.30, Family £13.50.

Cold War Jets Collection

Bruntingthorpe Aerodrome, Lutterworth, Leicestershire, LE17 5QS |
www.bruntingthorpeaviation.com

Complete Cold War era aircraft on display, including Lightnings, Victor, Comet 4, Buccaneers, Jet Provosts, Jaguar, Nimrod MRs, plus a Super Guppy and others. Aircraft are run down the runway on open day, usually in May and August.

Open Sundays 10am-4pm. See website for Open Days dates. Adults £5, accompanying child free.

Cornwall Aviation Heritage Centre

*HAS 3, Aerohub 2, St Mawgan, Newquay, Cornwall, TR8 4JN |
01637 861962 | www.cornwallaviationhc.co.uk*

A fantastic collection of complete aircraft, flyable in many cases. They include a Canberra, Sea Devon, VC-10, Hunters, Harrier, BAC One-Eleven and Varsity. Offers flight experiences.

Open daily except Saturday, 10.30am-4.30pm. Adults £7, Concessions £4, Children £4, Family £18.

de Havilland Aircraft Museum

*Salisbury Hall, London Colney, Hertfordshire, AL2 1BU |
www.dehavillandmuseum.co.uk*

Celebrating the history of this famous British aircraft designer and manufacturer. Exhibits include most de Havilland types, plus some of the larger designs including a Comet 1 and Trident 2E fuselage.

Open daily except Monday & Wednesday, plus public holidays, 10.30am-5pm, from March-late October. Adults £10, Seniors £8, Children £6, Family £25.

Dumfries & Galloway Aviation Museum

*Heathlands Industrial Estate, Dumfries, DG1 3PH |
01387 251623 | www.dumfriesaviationmuseum.com*

On the site of a former airfield. Collection is mostly military aircraft and helicopters, including Lightning, Canberra, Hunter, F-100 Sabre, Fairey Gannet. Also has forward section of Trident 3B and a Jetstream.

Open Wednesday 11am-4pm, Saturday-Sunday 10am-5pm (Easter-October). Also open Thursday & Friday 11am-4pm in July & August. Adults £4.50, Senior/Children £4, Family £12.50.

Duxford Imperial War Museum

Duxford, Cambridgeshire, CB22 4QR |
www.iwm.org.uk

A historic airfield and one of the country's best aircraft collections. Includes many historic warplanes, fighters, airliners, and an on-site American Air Museum with its own interesting aircraft. Airliners include Concorde, VC-10, Trident 2E, BAC One Eleven, Viscount, Herald and Bristol Britannia.

Open daily 10am-6pm. Adults £18, Concessions £14.40, Children £9, Family £47.25, Under 5s free.

East Midlands Aeropark

Castle Donington, Leicestershire, DE74, 2PR |
www.eastmidlandsaeropark.org

A small outdoor collection of historic aircraft including Canberra, Hunters, Nimrod, Buccaneer, Lightning, Vulcan, Argosy, Dove, Varsity, plus sections of Viscount, VC-10 and Vanguard.

Open Good Friday-31 October Saturday (12-5pm), Sunday (10.30am-5pm), Thursday (11am-4pm), public holidays (10.30am-5pm). Open 1 November-Good Friday Sunday (10.30am-5pm).

Adults £4, Children £2, Under 5s free.

FAST Museum

85 Farnborough Road, Farnborough, Hampshire, GU14 6TF |
01252 375050 | www.airsciences.org.uk

Dedicated to the Farnborough's contribution to air sciences and aviation history. Many exhibits, with a small collection of jets and helicopters outside.

Open Saturday, Sunday and public holidays, 10am-4pm. Free entry.

Fleet Air Arm Museum

RNAS Yeovilton, BA22 8HW |
01935 840565 | *www.fleetairarm.com*

Many aircraft and artefacts relating mostly to the Royal Navy and its history. Also houses one of the Concorde prototypes.

Open daily 10am-5.30pm (April-October), Wednesday-Sunday 10am-4.30pm (November-March). Adults £14, Concessions £12.50, Children £10.50, Under 5s free.

Jet Age Museum

Meteor Business Park, Cheltenham Road East, Gloucester, GL2 9QL |
www.jetagemuseum.org

A small museum at Gloucestershire Airport displaying mostly Gloster aircraft such as the Javelin and Meteor, plus sections of a Vulcan, Trident 3B and Typhoon.

Open Saturday- Sunday and public holidays, 10am-4pm.

Lincolnshire Aviation Heritage Centre

East Kirkby, Lincolnshire, PE23 4DE |
01790 763207 | *www.lincsaviation.co.uk*

Home to one of two operable Avro Lancasters in Britain. Does taxi runs with you on board! Also historic World War II base.

Open Monday-Saturday 9.30am-5pm (Easter-late October), 10am-4pm (late October-Easter). Adults £7.50, Seniors £6.50, Children £3, Family £20, Under 5's free.

Manchester Runway Visitor Park

Sunbank Lane, Altrincham, WA15 8XQ |
www.manchesterairport.co.uk

Widely used as a spotting location at Manchester Airport, the Runway Visitor Park is also home to a collection of aircraft including Avro RJX, Concorde, Trident 3B, Nimrod, and McDonnell Douglas DC-10 forward fuselage. Most are open to the public.

Open daily except 25-26 December from 8am. Closes 4pm (November-February), 6pm (March-May/September-October), 8pm (June-August). Free entry but car parking charges apply (£5-£12).

Midland Air Museum

Coventry Airport, Bagington, Warwickshire, CV3 4FR |
www.midlandairmuseum.co.uk

Nice outdoor collection include a Vulcan, Argosy, Viscount, Dove, Meter and many more aircraft from across the spectrum.

Open daily except 24-26 December, 10am-4.30pm (November-March), 10am-5pm (April-October).

Museum of Science and Industry

Liverpool Road, Manchester, M3 4FP |
www.msimanchester.org.uk

The Manchester museum has a hall full of aircraft of historic and scientific interest, including jets, bombers, gliders, airliners and light aircraft.

Open daily except 24-26 December and 1 January, 10am-5pm. Free entry.

National Museum of Flight

East Fortune Airfield, East Lothian, EH39 5LF, Scotland |
0300 123 6789 | www.nms.ac.uk/national-museum-of-flight

A significant aviation museum with many indoor and outdoor aircraft exhibits covering British aviation history in particular. Airliners on display include a Comet 4, BAC One-Eleven, Concorde, Dove and Twin Pioneer, plus forward sections of Boeing 707 and Trident 1C. Also many military and wartime aircraft.

Open daily 10am-5pm (late March-late October), Saturday-Sunday 10am-4pm (November-March). Adults £12, Senior £10, Children £7, Family £31, Under 5s free.

Newark Air Museum

Drove Lane, Newark, Nottinghamshire, NG24 2NY |
01636 707170 | www.newarkairmuseum.org

Large collection of significant aircraft, both civil and military, from early conflicts to recent times. Nicely presented in various hangars and outdoor areas.

Open daily except 24-26 & 31 December, 10am-5pm (March-October), 10am-4pm (November-February). Adults £8.50, Seniors £7.50, Children £4.50, Family £23, Under 5's free.

North East Land, Sea and Air Museum (NELSAM)

Old Washington Road, Sunderland, Tyne & Wear SR5 3HZ |
www.nelsam.org.uk

Hangar full of exhibits, mostly fighter jets and helicopters. Outside a Vulcan, Trident 1C, Lightning and Canberra. Also includes military vehicles and trams.

Open daily except 25, 26 and 31 December, 10am-5pm (April-October), 10am-dusk (November-March). Adults £5, Senior/Children £3, Family £13, Under 5s free.

Royal Air Force Museum Cosford

Shifnal, Shropshire, TF11 8UP |
01902 376 200 | www.rafmuseum.org.uk/cosford

A large museum with many interesting exhibits related to the history of the Royal Air Force. Mostly military aircraft, but also includes complete DC-3, Viscount, Britannia and Comet 1.

Open daily 10am-5pm (March-October),
10am-4pm (November-February). Free entry.

Royal Air Force Museum Hendon

Grahame Park Way, London, NW9 5LL |
020 8205 2266 | www.rafmuseum.org.uk/london

The other museum telling the history of the Royal Air Force with some significant aircraft and designs on display on the historic Hendon Airfield site. Includes Lancaster, Vulcan, B17G Flying Fortress, Spitfires, Hurricanes and many World War I aircraft.

Open daily 10am-6pm (March-October),
10am-5pm (November-February). Free entry.

Science Museum, London

Exhibition Road, South Kensington, London, SW7 2DD |
www.sciencemuseum.org.uk

Large museum in central London. The aviation hall has a number of complete aircraft and sections to explain the history and science of flight.

Open daily, 10am-7pm. Free entry.

Science Museum, Wroughton

Red Barn, Wroughton, Swindon, Wilstshire, SN4 9LT |
www.sciencemuseum.org.uk

Acting as a store for the Science Museum's largest collections, it comprises many complete aircraft and airliners, including Lockheed Constellation, Boeing 247, Douglas DC-3, Trident 3B, Comet 4B.

Open Fridays 10am-5pm. Visits by appointment only.

Solway Aviation Museum

Carlisle Airport, Cumbria, CA6 4NW |
01228 573823 | *www.solway-aviation-museum.co.uk*

Mostly military collection, with complete Vulcan, Canberra, Hunter, Lightning, Phantom. Trident 1C cockpit.

Open: Fri, Sat, Sun and public holidays from late March-late October. Adults £6, Senior/Child £4, Family £15.

The Helicopter Museum

Locking Moor Road, Weston-Super-Mare, BS24 8PP |
01934 635227 | *www.helicoptermuseum.co.uk*

The largest dedicated helicopter museum in the world. Displays around 80 examples across the spectrum from around the world.

Open Wednesday-Sunday plus public holidays, 10am-5.30pm (April-October), 10am-4.30pm (November-March). Adults £7, Senior £6, Children £4.50, Family £19/20.

The Shuttleworth Collection

Old Warden Aerodrome, Bedfordshire, SG18 9EP |
01767 627 927 | www.shuttleworth.org

Britain's premier collection of flyable vintage aeroplanes, mostly from World War I era. The collection often takes part in air displays, particularly at its Old Warden home. When not flying visitors can see them at close quarters.

Open daily 9.30am-5pm (February-October), 10am-4pm (November-February). Check event dates on website. Admission prices depend on whether visit coincides with an event or access to Swiss Garden.

Yorkshire Air Museum

Elvington, York, YO41 4AU |
01904 608595 | www.yorkshireairmuseum.org

Occupying the wartime part of Elvington Aerodrome, with many of the historic buildings preserved. Aircraft occupy various hangars, ranging from World War I types to Cold War jets. Highlights include Douglas DC-3, Avro Victor, Nimrod, Halifax and Mosquito. Some aircraft are taxied on occasion.

Open daily except 25-26 December and 1 January,
10am-4pm (Winter), 10am-5pm (Summer).

Also by the Author

Handley Page Herald Timelines
ISBN: 978-0-9930950-1-6

The Herald was an innovative British airliner which started life as a piston aircraft and had to be quickly reimagined to utilise turboprop engines in order to keep up with the competition. This book tells the story of the Herald from its inception through to its entry into service, the airlines that operated it, and the remaining examples today.

World Airports Spotting Guides
978-0-9930950-3-0

Detailed spotting guides to over 300 worldwide airports. Find out exactly where to watch aircraft, where to take photographs, and what kind of aircraft you'll see there. Includes spotting hotels, museums and other attractions.

Airport Spotting Hotels
ISBN: 978-0-9930950-6-1

Make the most of every trip by finding a room at an airport hotel with a view. Airport Spotting Hotels details over 270 hotels in 54 countries that offer views of aircraft movements, including details of the best rooms and what you'll see.

Lightning Source UK Ltd.
Milton Keynes UK
UKHW021112091118
332056UK00005B/99/P